QUIXOTE

QUIXOTE

THE NOVEL AND THE WORLD

ILAN STAVANS

 W. W. NORTON & COMPANY   New York | London

For information about permission to reproduce selections from this book,
write to Permissions, W. W. Norton & Company, Inc.,
500 Fifth Avenue, New York, NY 10110

For information about special discounts for bulk purchases, please contact
W. W. Norton Special Sales at specialsales@wwnorton.com or 800-233-4830

Manufacturing by RR Donnelley, Harrisonburg
Book design by Chris Welch
Production manager: Devon Zahn

Library of Congress Cataloging-in-Publication Data

Stavans, Ilan.
Quixote : the novel and the world / Ilan Stavans. — First edition.
pages cm
Includes bibliographical references and index.
ISBN 978-0-393-08302-6 (hardcover)
1. Cervantes Saavedra, Miguel de, 1547–1616. Don Quixote. 2. Cervantes Saavedra,
Miguel de, 1547–1616. Don Quixote—Influence. I. Title.
PQ6352.S73 2015
863'.3—dc23
2015013784

W. W. Norton & Company, Inc.
500 Fifth Avenue, New York, NY 10110
www.wwnorton.com

W. W. Norton & Company Ltd., Castle House,
75/76 Wells Street, London W1T 3QT

1 2 3 4 5 6 7 8 9 0

To my parents,
Ofelia and Abraham—
soñadores.
And to my siblings,
Darián and Liora.

CONTENTS

CLASSIC: A book people praise but don't read.

—Mark Twain, *Following the Equator* (1897)

PREFACE

steroid 3552 displays some bizarre, disassociated behavior. Astronomers describe it as a small body orbiting around the sun. Yet it acts like a comet and, for that matter, like an extinct one, meaning that the asteroid has expelled from its nucleus most of its volatile ice. Thus, it is lifeless, incapable of generating energy in its tail—a comet without force, a kind of impostor, pretending to be something it isn't.

Aside from its number, astronomers have given it a name: Don Quixote. Greek myths are often used to name planets (Mars, Jupiter, Saturn, etc.) as well as asteroids (Apollo, Trojan, Centaur, etc.). The names of other such chunks of space matter have also been drawn from writers' names (Franz Kafka and Kurt Vonnegut, for example) and literary characters (the moons orbiting Uranus are named after characters in Shakespeare's plays). The asteroid known as Don Quixote was detected by Swiss astronomer Paul Wild in 1983. Measuring almost twelve miles in diameter (the width of San Francisco Bay), it has an inclined comet-like path, crosses the Mars orbit, and is frequently perturbed by Jupiter's gravitational force. Its existence is tenuous: at some point, like other debris in the solar system, it might crash into the sun. But it could escape such a tragic end.

In other words, Don Quixote is likely to wander forever—whatever that word means in our vast, expanding universe. Isn't that what the real Don Quixote, the character created by Miguel de Cervantes Saavedra, does too—wander around aimlessly in our imagination? Personally, I find it fitting to call Asteroid 3552 after what is arguably the most famous—and, in my view, the best—novelistic character of all time. He too is a kind of impostor, a migrating object faking his path through existence, an artifact passing for something he is not, dreaming of an alternative life.

We all dream of a different life. We all want to be someone else. Don Quixote is such an appealing character because he acts on that dream. As a result, he is seen as a fool, imprisoned in his own self-made universe. But contrary to common wisdom, *foolishness* isn't the antonym of *reason*. One can be a wise fool as well as an insane genius. Reason and foolishness—call it madness!—are actually one and the same: to be who we want to be, we need to invent a self, complete with its own logic. To be free, we need to create our own definition of liberty.

Looking back, I realize that I have spent my entire adult life wanting to be Don Quixote. Or, rather, imitating him. I have created a self that feels appropriate, a sense of freedom I am comfortable inhabiting. I have sought to be a quixotic fool.

My admiration for *Don Quixote of La Mancha* has taken myriad forms. In my library, I have a large collection of *Quixotalia*—for example, versions of the novel in multiple languages (from Yiddish to Korean, from Quechua to Klingon). I also have an endless assortment of artifacts inspired by it: films and recordings of theater productions, action figures, picture books, lunch boxes, lithographs, advertisements, and postal stamps. Ironically, they all mimic a hero whose existence is spent as an impostor, pretending to be someone else.

Aside from collecting all sorts of tchotchkes, I've been rereading the novel, as William Faulkner often said he did: about once a year, forever learning from its protagonist. I have also taught it countless times to passionate, devoted students eager to find out why the darned book is so long and why it has remained a classic over so many centuries. Their research has pushed me in endless directions: What makes Picasso's minimalist depiction of the knight-errant and his squire—no more than a handful of pencil lines—enduring? How do we explain Orson Welles's fascination with it? Why did George Washington like the character so much? Did Cantinflas, the so-called Hispanic Charlie Chaplin, help to popularize the novel more than anyone else in the twentieth century? And is there a reason why translators like François Filleau de Saint-Martin dreamed of adding extra chapters to it?

I first discovered *Don Quixote* when I was in my teens, still living in Mexico, where I grew up. My very first copy, a cheap Spanish-language paperback, ended up in the garbage. I must have tried reading it but found it untidy, unfocused, and monotonous—in short, impenetrable. Why keep an item you do not like? So I threw it away in the bathroom's wastebasket. I can still see it at the bottom, amid used Q-tips, an empty toothpaste box, and Kleenex.

In 1980, I bought myself another single-volume copy (the First and Second Parts together in a hardcover edition). I know the exact year because I used to engrave my full name—Ilan Stavchansky—in my books using a special metal-press seal I had bought through the mail. The seal had a coat of arms I had designed, and under it, I signed in Hebrew and added the year.

Why such an obsession to claim this copy as my own? Perhaps because of the quick, miserable death the earlier *Don Quixote* had received. Released by the publisher Bruguera in Barcelona in 1974, my embossed copy was part of the sixth printing (in Spanish, printings are called editions) and was bound in a handsome black cover that looked like expensive leather. It was by no means a collector's copy, although it proved durable. It came with me to New York when I emigrated, moving from one apartment to the next as I made my way through life.

Youth is both an illness and its cure. I was infatuated with the decaying state of the world and wanted to change it, while being perfectly aware of the impracticalities of my dream. For one thing, I wanted to one day become a writer. Writers spend their time in isolation, putting words on a page. How much more impractical might one be? Cervantes's novel turns those impracticalities into a quest. Its protagonist is a hidalgo, a nobleman, who is around fifty years old and doesn't do much except read escapist literature. Soon his brains dry up. He starts fashioning himself as a knight-errant eager to fight oppression, even though the "injustices" he encounters are imagined and his attempts to right them ineffective. Everything he does is pathetic.

That, precisely, is what I adored about the book: its vitality as well as its pathetic nature. Alonso Quijano, the hidalgo, concocts for himself a ridiculous name. He finds shining armor in the closet. He turns his skinny horse into Rocinante, a name befitting the illustrious horses of mythical stature that accompany adventurers like Amadis of Gaul and Tirant lo Blanc. And he identifies a humble village woman, Aldonza Lorenzo, as his beautiful and virtuous dame. His imagination alone launches him on an adventure that requires him to be courageous.

Isn't that what we all do in life: find a purpose, a mission, to justify our days? As a young man, I admired Don Quixote because of his idealism. But as I've returned to the book time and again, I have found other sources of inspiration. Maybe the plot isn't really about an idealist but instead a fool. After all, one doesn't reach fifty and find nothing else to do but rectify all wrongs if insanity isn't a part of it. As I myself have reached the age of Cervantes's protagonist, I realize that this is the story of a middle-aged quest, as the body deteriorates, to retrieve the dreams we nurtured earlier in life.

In Spanish, the novel is affectionately referred to as *El Quijote*, and I shall also use that title here unless I'm referring to an English translation of it. The article *el* means "the"; in other words, this is it, the one and only, the novel of novels. The accolades it has received over the centuries are unparalleled. Charles-Augustin Sainte-Beuve called it "the Bible of humanity." Lionel Trilling stated that "all prose fiction is a variation on the theme of *Don Quixote*." Tom Sawyer makes a reference to the enchantment at the heart of *El Quijote* in chapter 3 of the *Adventures of Huckleberry Finn*.

The novel argues that reality is a concoction, that what we see isn't there but is what we want to see. Therefore, it is said that Cervantes legitimized subjectivity, that he endorsed a world where truth is no longer absolute. It has also been argued that Cervantes's magnum opus gave traction to the Enlightenment, that it begat modernity, teaching us the meaning of anxiety, the sense of being adrift in the world, without direction, trapped in the prison of our own individual loneliness. Jorge Luis Borges argued that Cervantes raises his character to the status of "a demigod in our consciousness." He added, "Don Quixote is the only solitude that occurs in world literature."

It is not only widely regarded as the best novel but also the most popular. At the dawn of the twenty-first century, the Norwegian Academy of Science and Letters asked a hundred writers from just about everywhere on the globe to name what in their estimation was the best novel. *El Quijote* won by a landslide: fifty respondents named it their favorite. Indeed, it is the runaway best seller in fiction, with millions of copies sold annually around the globe. Only the Bible outdoes it, but, then again, the Bible wasn't written by a single author. And not all of us describe it as fiction.

Trilling's view that "all prose fiction is a variation on the theme of *Don Quixote*" revolves around the fact that the novel as a genre makes an attempt at verisimilitude—the likeness or semblance of a narrative to reality—and that, in *El Quijote*, that verisimilitude is at once a triumph and a defeat because Cervantes delivers the adventures of a madman who thinks he isn't actually mad. Indeed, everyone has a theory about what makes Cervantes's book tick. Some argue that the novel is a psychiatric treatise in disguise. Others suggest it is a celebration of reason. Arguments have even been made that the novel is a cautionary tale against the excesses of religion and that

Don Quixote is a doppelgänger of Jesus Christ. Furthermore, there are commentators who describe Cervantes's approach to his characters as bullying, not to say condescending, whereas an army of defenders portray his approach as utterly humane.

Such is the magic *El Quijote* exerts on people that it forces us to consider what a classic is. Definitions abound: a classic is a book that defies the passing of time, or perhaps one confirming that time is never static; a book that is actually many books, as many as the number of readers it has; a book capable of shaping a nation; or a book whose obvious imperfections are kindly brushed aside in favor of its felicities, which are as substantial as they are enduring. There are other definitions of the classic I want to make: a book that is a mirror in which we see ourselves reflected; a book that accumulates interpretations; a book in which we meet readers not only from the present but also from the past and the future.

What is the color of Emma Bovary's eyes? Depending on which chapter readers find themselves in, brown, black, or blue. How many daughters does Tevye the Dairyman have? Five, seven, twelve . . . Likewise, *El Quijote* is clumsy in a number of ways. Indeed, I sometimes imagine the manuscript, fresh from Cervantes's pen, landing today on the desk of a New York City book editor. It is an entertaining game. For the fun of it, let's say it arrives first in English translation. The editor pretends to read it, then dispatches this rejection letter:

> Dear Señor Michael of Sirvientes:
> We've now had the chance to read the long manuscript—
> a behemoth, really—you kindly sent us. While we appreciate your earnest attempt at developing the distinct

personalities of the old chap and his fat servant, we've found the storyline to be problematic. You stuff the novel with one too many adventures that do little to advance the plot, which suffers, as a result, from lack of direction and cohesion. There are too many characters whose fate the reader gets attached to but who suddenly disappear never to be heard from again. Maybe another publisher will be willing to trim the book to approximately three hundred pages; we simply don't have the staff to invest in such a task.

Plus, what is one to make of the fact that Cide Hamette Beneguelli is said to be the true creator of the book? Is this true? At times this seems like an ingenious device. However, our legal department forbids us to bring out a novel whose authorship is uncertain—we would be wide open to a lawsuit over copyright.

If you decide to revise the novel before submitting it elsewhere, we advise you to look closely at the style to avoid convoluted sentences, overreliance on a limited vocabulary, questionable use of adjectives, and other careless errors.

While *Don Quixote* is not really for us, we do wish you success in placing it elsewhere. Let me conclude by saying that should you have something substantially shorter, preferably with some elements of Magical Realism, please don't hesitate to send it to us.

Yours sincerely,

This imaginary editor is right: *El Quijote* is at once long and long-winded. The author's pen is often in overdrive, figuring, disfiguring, and reconfiguring the Spanish landscape in ways that verge on the unreliable. There are obvious inconsistencies. And the language is at times flat, even uninspired.

Still, those who love *El Quijote* as I do love it beyond compare. We see it as a life manual, a variation on a quote by Terence— "*Homo sum, humani nihil a me alienum puto*" becomes "Nothing human is alien to this book"—for, like *Hamlet*, it contains the universe in a nutshell and imagines itself covering infinite space. Coleridge recommended it to anyone who would listen.

El Quijote was published in two parts, the first in 1605 (referred to as *princeps*), the second in 1615. I am not fully of the opinion that a work of art is independent of its creator, although somehow that approach is alluring to me. There are a number of commentators—from Miguel de Unamuno to Jorge Luis Borges—who believe Cervantes is an ancillary player in the story of how the novel came to be, that without him we would still have this magnificent book. I'm in disagreement with this stance, yet I don't want to push the opposite approach either: that this is an autobiographical novel. Sure, there are autobiographical elements in it. What matters to me, though, is what *El Quijote* delivers: the flux of the narrative, its durability.

In THIS SHORT BOOK, I start with the local (stressing the universal) and move to the global (emphasizing the particular).

In Section One, "The Novel," I look at the components that make *El Quijote* what it is: a self-reflective labyrinthine narrative. I start with Cervantes on his deathbed in Madrid on April 22, 1616 (the same year Shakespeare died). I then move on to what we know biographically about him, then meditate on his career, although I mostly focus on his magnum opus. I analyze Cervantes's artistic concerns, the political, religious, and cultural tensions that shaped him. Spain during the corrupt monarchies of Philip II, king of Castile, and his inept son, King Philip III, was an intolerant place. I explore the role played by the Holy Office of the Inquisition as a tool against the Counter-Reformation and the mythology of Cervantes's novel as a paragon of liberty and an instrument in the modern fight against censorship, which are, to some extent, accurate depictions, although *El Quijote* also naively suggests that censorship is good—that is, useful—to literature.

One of Cervantes's lasting contributions is the plasticity of his language. I reflect on the development of Castilian, the language that defined the Spanish monarchy in 1492. I meditate on the aesthetics of "the baroque mind" that colored the arts in *El Siglo de Oro*, as the Spanish Golden Age is often referred to—a period encompassing a couple hundred years and devoted to the investigation of the mind's tricks, starting precisely the moment Columbus sailed the Atlantic Ocean and ending in 1681 with the death of its last famous practitioner, Pedro Calderón de la Barca, author of *Life Is a Dream* (1635). I ponder the concept of *limpieza de sangre*, purity of blood, among hidalgos. Cervantes, it is sometimes insinuated, might have had Jewish blood, although no clear evidence exists to prove it. Still, the provocative first line of *El Quijote*—"*En un lugar de la Mancha, de cuyo nombre no quiero acordarme, no ha mucho tiempo que vivía un hidalgo de los de lanza en astillero, adarga antigua, rocín flaco y galgo corredor,*" In a village of La Mancha, the name of which I have no desire to call to mind, there lived not long since one of those gentlemen that keep a lance in the lance-rack, an old buckler, a lean hack, and a greyhound for coursing—hides as much as it reveals about the identity of the protagonist, Alonso Quijano, which might be a comment on the veil certain noblemen in the early seventeenth century used in order not to attract undue attention from the authorities: silence as a shield to protect privacy. I also discuss the role of Muslim culture in Cervantes's time and his provocative use of a fictional Arab historian to joke about the twisted origins of Iberian ancestry.

At one point, seeking to map Cervantes's affinities, I reduce the novel to a set of basic numbers: how many letters it contains, how many and what types of words. This allows me to consider the overall reach of Cervantes's lexicon. In line with Sigmund Freud, I ask if it might be possible to diagnose Alonso Quijano's illness from a psychiatric perspective. Is he schizophrenic or manic-depressive? I discuss the way Don Quixote and Sancho Panza are shaped as an odd couple; the "ghost-like" role played by Dulcinea del Toboso; the novel's parody on chivalry; the mechanics of its famous first line; and the metafictional aspects overall that are built like Russian nesting dolls, one story within another story, and so on. In this regard I analyze how, along with a handful of other representative European works from the end of the fifteenth century, *El Quijote* is seen as an engine of the Enlightenment. I also talk about the route Don Quixote and Sancho take, physical and spiritual, and the creation of Barataria, the island Sancho is made governor of, as a conduit for Cervantes's observations about the Spanish incursion into the New World. And I talk about the adjective *quijotesco*, which has become an essential component of the Hispanic worldview.

Section Two, "The World," follows the vertiginous speed at which *El Quijote* became larger than life, a platform of arrival and departure, a center of gravity for all Western literature —the universe bounded in a nutshell, its readers counting themselves kings of infinite space. I use the military defeat Spain suffered against the British in 1588, almost two decades before Cervantes wrote the First Part, to explore the theme of loss for Spain of its colonies across the Atlantic Ocean, which *El Quijote*, for better or worse, has come to represent. I begin this section with a disquisition on how Cervantes's book gave rise to an ideology known as *Quijotismo* and how that ideology played out during various historical periods in Spanish history, especially—through the works of Unamuno and José Ortega y Gasset—at the end of the nineteenth century during the Spanish-American War of 1898, when the country ceded control of its satellites in the Caribbean Basin and the Philippines. The novel then inspired a series of homages in the Hispanic world, direct or otherwise, that culminated in what came to be known as *Menardismo*, the capacity to be creative in a landscape defined by unoriginality. In Latin America, it is a book for all seasons, which means everyone finds in it what they're looking for, even if that find is apocryphal. For instance, a defiant line from it—*"Ladran, Sancho, señal que cabalgamos,"* They are barking, Sancho, proof that we're still riding forward—has often been quoted by politicians like Eva Perón and Hugo Chávez, as well as writers and artists, even though it is nowhere to be found in the novel.

The second section of this book then moves to an even larger stage. Quantitatively, the number of adaptations of *El Quijote* in literature, chess sets, and so on is endless. I first focus on

the elements that unite Cervantes and Shakespeare, the two
giants of the European Renaissance. I explore the way German
Romantics, such as Goethe and Richard Strauss, idealized the
story, and I address the countless ways the novel, as a popular icon in mass culture, inspired lithographers like Gustave
Doré and Expressionist painters like Picasso. I then reflect on
its adaptations into music, opera, theater, film, and even video
games. I compare *El Quijote* to Gustave Flaubert's *Madame
Bovary*, talk about Fyodor Dostoyevsky's infatuation with the
novel, and discuss Franz Kafka's famous parable in which
Sancho is the actual creator of Don Quixote, as well as Jorge
Luis Borges's influential short story, "Pierre Menard, Author of
the *Quixote*," in which a nineteenth-century French Symbolist
attempts to rewrite—not copy but rewrite—Cervantes's novel.
I meditate on the vicissitudes of *El Quijote* in translation,
concentrating on the knight-errant's adventures in English,
a language in which there are more than twenty full-fledged
renditions, some of which I compare and contrast. And I pay
special attention to the novel's reception in the United States,
from the Founding Fathers to William Cullen Bryant and
James Russell Lowell, from Herman Melville to Mark Twain,
from John Steinbeck to Susan Sontag. I talk about the Broadway musical *Man of La Mancha*, especially about its theme song,
"The Impossible Dream," and even discuss an episode of *The
Muppet Show*.

There are travel agencies making their livelihood on *El Quijote*, as is a supermarket chain in Japan. Academic conferences
have been devoted to a single word from the novel, cookbooks
and clothing lines have been inspired by it, and political parties
have built their gravitas on the knight-errant's resilience. Along

the way, I discuss Manuel de Falla, María Amparo Ruiz de Burton and György Lukács, Georg Philipp Telemann and Michel Foucault, Erasmus of Rotterdam and George Balanchine, and José Guadalupe Posada.

In spite of the collection of *Quixotalia* I have amassed through the years, this overabundance of novel-related stuff still seems rather implausible to me. Even more implausible is that Cervantes wasn't far from his death when he completed the book's final scene. That is, he could have died without finishing it, which means we would have been left without the source from which we drink every day. And yet, he managed to make Alonso Quijano repent his sins, refute his lifelong delusions of chivalric grandeur, and die peacefully in his own bed.

The history of how *El Quijote* became an international sensation is also the history of how Western civilization came to terms with its artistic vision. This book, then, is an invitation to engage in cultural history that traces *El Quijote*'s path from the surprising success it became in early-seventeenth-century Spain to the global moneymaking machine it is now. My purpose is to explain how Cervantes, a second-rate poet and dramaturge of modest esteem, became, along with his contemporaries Shakespeare and Montaigne, the unlikely father of modernity.

El Quijote makes me proud of having been born into the Spanish language. In fact, I am convinced that the Spanish language exists in order for this magisterial novel to inhabit it. Hispanic civilization—its people, its culture, its politics— would not be what it is without *El Quijote*. Simultaneously, I counterargue that, against common perceptions, classics have no nationality. As the reader will find out, these two statements are not incompatible.

THE NOVEL

SECTION ONE

IN HIS LIKENESS

hen Miguel de Cervantes Saavedra died in Madrid at the age of sixty-eight on the evening of April 22, 1616, and his remains were buried in an unmarked grave at the Convent of the Barefoot Trinitarians (Trinitarias Descalzas), few—not even Cervantes himself, in spite of his reputation as the "Prince of Wits"—predicted that his work would have a secure place on the bookshelf of classics. It is true that the First Part of his magnum opus, *El ingenioso hidalgo don Quijote de la Mancha*—in English *The Ingenious Hidalgo Don Quixote of la Mancha*—had achieved a *succès d'estime* that reached far and wide. But in early-seventeenth-century Spain, the novel wasn't considered as prestigious as other literary genres, such as the *comedia*, a favorite of theater-goers, or the sonnet, a poetic form that elicited obsessive devotion among lovers of prosody.

This novel in particular was a spoof; that is, it was not considered a serious work of artistic expression. Plus, Cervantes was known as a playwright of modest talent, not as celebrated as Félix Arturo Lope de Vega y Carpio, who was known as the "Phoenix of Wits" and author of nearly eighteen hundred *comedias* and three thousand sonnets, few of which survive today. Nor did Cervantes's sonnets or other poetic exercises, also seen as tame in comparison to those by such figures as Francisco de Quevedo and Luis de Góngora, grant him a secure place among his literary peers. Though today the Spanish government offers the annual Premio Cervantes to honor the lifetime achievement of an outstanding writer in the Spanish language, an award that frequently goes to figures whose work coheres with the intellectual status quo, it is unlikely that Cervantes himself would have been the recipient of such an award. It was Lope de Vega, in fact, who, commenting on the writers on whose oeuvre readers needed to keep an eye on the upcoming year (1604, though the date is debatable), mercilessly stated, "None is as bad as Cervantes."

The overall plot of *El Quijote* is rather easy to summarize, although any summary of it inevitably feels reductive, even stilted. A fiftyish hidalgo by the name of Alonso Quijano (also known as Quijana, Quijada, and Quesada), living in a hacienda in an unknown place in the region of La Mancha in central Spain, has been spending his days reading novels of chivalry, marvel-filled cycles of narratives, extremely popular among aristocratic readers, written in prose or verse and based on fantastic legends that featured a masculine hero, a knight-errant who embarks on a quest while usually declaring Platonic love for his dame. The word *hidalgo* comes from *fidalgo*. According to lore, it means *hijo de algo*, child of someone. In truth, it refers to a member of the lower nobility. It might also refer to someone whose ancestry was defined by purity of blood, that is, one who came from a family of old Christians.

In Spain at the time, there were different kinds of hidalgos, as listed in the *Diccionario de la Real Academia Española* (*DRAE*), including the *hidalgo de ejecutoria*, someone whose blood lineage makes him such, and the *hidalgo de privilegio*, a person whose position is acquired through money or privilege. The novel's narrator doesn't offer any further detail. The reader is simply told that the protagonist is a hidalgo who lives with his niece, who is under twenty; a female housekeeper, who is past forty; and a lad who does the field work. That this hidalgo is on good terms with the town's priest and barber. And that he doesn't attend to the affairs of his hacienda because he spends all his time reading. Indeed, such is his habit that, in John Ormsby's English translation (hereafter used, unless stated otherwise), published in London in 1885, we are told:

> He became so absorbed in his books that he spent his nights from sunset to sunrise, and his days from dawn to dark, poring over them; and what with little sleep and much reading his brains got so dry that he lost his wits.

Having "lost his wits," Alonso Quijano suddenly convinces himself he is a knight-errant like Palmerin of England and Amadis of Gaul. Persuading himself that his mission in life is to correct all of the world's ills, he comes up with the heroic name of Don Quixote of La Mancha, turns the beautiful village girl Aldonza Lorenzo into his lady Dulcinea del Toboso, and identifies a commoner known as Sancho Panza as his squire and loyal companion.

All these events are conveyed in just a few early pages. The rest of the plot is composed of Don Quixote's serendipitous adventures. He travels as far as Barcelona on the Mediterranean Sea. In total, he has three expeditions, from which he invariably comes back to his hacienda beaten up and in questionable health. In a famous episode, he fights against windmills, thinking they are giants. In another, he frees some prisoners, only to be beaten up by them. In another episode, he faces a fierce African lion being transported in a cage. In yet another, he enters a mysterious cave and watches a puppet show, only to destroy the whole set in a rage because one of the characters in the show is being abused and he wants to correct that wrong. Then, in reward for Sancho's services, Don Quixote promises him the governorship of the fictional island Barataria, which becomes real toward the conclusion of the novel. And, in the longest episode in the Second Part, the knight-errant and his squire are hosted in a castle by the Duke and the Duchess, where, in carnivalesque fashion, they are ridiculed by everyone.

There is no better way to describe *El Quijote* than as an intermittent, discontinuous series of adventures unified—at times rather tenuously—by the presence of Don Quixote and Sancho. I say tenuously because Cervantes's novel is interrupted by small, novella-length subplots, some of which are told by secondary characters to the knight-errant and his squire, who become mere spectators, as disengaged as the book's reader. Throughout the narrative, the tension between what is real and what is imagined, what the actual world presents and what Don Quixote sees, is the engine moving the action forward. In his desire to bring justice to a society marked by inequality, immorality, and corruption, the knight-errant is convinced that the world, his as well as ours, is controlled by enchanters, especially Friston the Magician, the most sneaky of them all.

These magicians mean to undermine Don Quixote's quest for justice. As the storyline progresses, various supporting characters, in order to subdue Don Quixote and appease his desire to subvert the status quo, pretend they too exist in his imaginary universe, being knights themselves, as well as princesses and other mythical types. In the end, Alonso Quijano surrenders his identity as Don Quixote and, on his deathbed, apologizes for the endless sequence of mishaps he put others through.

In spite of its flaws, *El Quijote*, a parody of chivalry novels—those very novels that led Don Quixote to madness—gained popularity because it announced the dawn of a new era in which the hero was no longer superhuman. Instead, he was portrayed as vulnerable, imperfect, and, therefore, human in all his frailties. Novels of chivalry were to early modern Europe of the sixteenth century what thrillers are to our age. The Italian *Espejo de caballerías*, translated into Spanish by Pedro López de Santa Catalina, the Portuguese *Palmerín de Inglaterra* by Moraes, the native Iberian *Belianís de Grecia* by Fernández, and countless other chivalry titles, either imported or made for national consumption, fed an insatiable hunger. Cervantes opened his book with spin-off poems dedicated to some of these favorites, such as this sonnet supposedly written by Amadis of Gaul to Don Quixote:

> Thou that didst imitate that life of mine
> When I in lonely sadness on the great
> Rock Pena Pobre sat disconsolate,
> In self-imposed penance there to pine;
>
> Thou, whose sole beverage was the bitter brine
> Of thine own tears, and who withouten plate

Of silver, copper, tin, in lowly state
Off the bare earth and on earth's fruits didst dine;

Live thou, of thine eternal glory sure.
So long as on the round of the fourth sphere
The bright Apollo shall his coursers steer,

In thy renown thou shalt remain secure,
Thy country's name in story shall endure,
And thy sage author stand without a peer.

Novels of chivalry adhere to a basic five-step formula: one, an open-ended structure, whereby a hero's adventures are prolonged in book after book, similar to the Sherlock Holmes or James Bond series; two, the devotion to an idealized woman to whom the hero declares his Platonic love, expressed through his actions on the battlefield; three, a Christian concept of pride and honor against the infidels, who depend on enchantment to succeed in their treacherous tasks; four, the lost manuscript, through which the story of the extraordinary hero could be accessed directly, and without which the narrative resorts to an accumulation of indirect accounts; and five, the setting in an imaginary geography filled with enchanted castles, dragons, monsters, and other chimeras.

Spanish civilization itself is built on the myth of a knight, Rodrigo Díaz de Vivar, alias *El Cid Campeador*, an eleventh-century Christian crusader and emblem of valor on which the knight-errant tradition is based. El Cid is said to have fought against the Moors, his former allies, advancing a process that ultimately resulted in an attempt at the unification of Spain under the Catholic monarchs Isabella and Ferdinand in 1492. Though El Cid's odyssey is rooted in historical fact, he and the other knights of chivalry literature are invariably fictitious.

Lord Byron said that *El Quijote* "smiled Spain's chivalry away." Parody was Cervantes's way of giving new life to archetypical characters that had become stilted from overuse. The protagonists, the knight-errant and his squire, aren't cartoonish; instead they are made of flesh and bone. Alonso Quijano lives with a niece and a housekeeper. At first he is portrayed as reclusive, with little interest in social interactions. His horse, Rocinante, is frail. Sancho Panza has a wife and children and is an uneducated villager who dreams of becoming the governor of an island. Neither he nor Don Quixote is fit for the road, let alone for battle. Unlike the characters created by Amadis of Gaul and other chivalry authors, Don Quixote and Sancho suffer inner doubts. *El Quijote*, after all, is a forerunner of the nineteenth-century *bildungsroman*, a novel of education, a novel about the quest for self-definition.

Such comedic depiction of social affairs quickly became a favorite of readers worldwide because they saw in it a vivid assessment of human folly. In the first decade of the seventeenth century, the nation had just entered a new political era. Philip II, also called Philip the Prudent, a member of the House of Habsburg, died in 1598. He was an autocrat who negotiated the nation's *morisco* (e.g., Christians of Moorish descent) problem by forcing the remaining Muslim population to convert to Christianity, which sometimes resulted in revolt. He further burdened the empire with debt and brought about astronomical inflation. The Armada had been magisterially defeated more than a couple of decades prior. The Spanish Empire was in disarray, and there was a general mistrust of the nation, its political quagmire, its economic gambles, in European circles. The roots of anti-Hispanism, a negative response to all things Iberian from Spain's American colonies, were also established in this period.

The person in charge of sending the manuscript to the printer was Francisco de Robles. The publisher was Juan de la Cuesta. The first printing of *El Quijote*, also known as the *princeps*, considered by *Cervantistas* to be the official publication of the First Part of Cervantes's novel, was of eighteen hundred copies in 1605. The printing took years to sell out. Still, it seems to have caught on because pirated editions quickly showed up in Valencia and Aragón in Spain, as well as in Lisbon, Portugal. It is known that copies of the novel also made it as a kind of *samizdat* to the New World, where the Holy Office of the Inquisition had banned novels—fiction in general—for dangerously promoting paganism. The knight and his squire soon became fixtures of festivals as costumed figures, effigies, and wooden sculptures paraded through the streets of Mexico and Peru. Yet Cervantes's contract, in retrospect at least, appears to have been rather lousy. When he died, not long after the publication of the Second Part, his assets and those of his family were almost nonexistent.

Likewise, neither the manuscript of *El Quijote* nor the proofs survived. This is unnerving to *Cervantistas* eager to understand the method the author used to compose the novel. Did he have a preconceived plan? Was there a journal he found helpful during the composition? Were there numerous drafts? Did he cross out words, lines, entire paragraphs? We don't have manuscripts of any of his other books either, among them *La Galatea* (1585) and *Voyage to Parnassus* (1614), or his *entremeses*, his brief one-act theater pieces, often performed before a play.

About a hundred typos were corrected in the *princeps*. But other problems weren't as easily solvable since they relate to the novel's structure and the author's disposition. For instance, at several points the novel includes entire subplots—actually, autonomous novellas, such as *The Ill-Conceived Curiosity* and *The Captive's Tale*—which, as readers frequently point out, have little connection to the novel's central theme. The author, in a moment of laziness, seems to have taken these manuscripts out of a drawer and inserted them. Scholars do not take these to be full-fledged mistakes. They are more like detours, typical of premodern literature, where storytelling was not understood as a straight line between point A and point Z. These novellas have their charm. If pushed to find meaning in them, a savvy reader will intuitively link them to something in the overall narrative arc.

As for what one might describe as glaring mistakes, the most often discussed is the impossibility of Sancho's donkey being stolen in one scene (First Part, chapter XXV) and reappearing soon thereafter, without explanation. Another one relates to the various names of Sancho in the First Part (e.g., Sancho Zancas) as well as his wife's different names (standardized, finally, as Teresa Panza). Obvious mistakes aside, the most unwieldy problem in *El Quijote*, aside from its length, is its stylistic carelessness. Cervantes was not a meticulous craftsman. His sentences go on and on and on and on, and so on. An idea that might be summarized is expanded without reason.

Some of these inconsistencies might be owed to the fact that Cervantes didn't have a copy-editor or editor responsible for overseeing the entire manuscript. In the early seventeenth century, there were *correctores*, typographers in charge of spotting obvious printing errors, but they weren't in charge of streamlining the manuscript. We might guess his mistakes are the result of haste, that he was impatient, even impulsive. But these are only guesses.

It is quite possible that, barring the existence of *El Quijote*, Cervantes would not be remembered today. Centuries after his death, he remains an enigma. As in the case of Shakespeare, his contemporary (under the Julian calendar, they died the same day), material related to Cervantes's life is extraordinarily scarce. What we do know is recorded in a handful of useful, recent biographies, such as the ones by William Byron (1978) and Jean Canavaggio (1991), and also gleaned from the unreadable, multivolume "life" written by Luis Astrana Marín during the early period of the Francisco Franco regime, between 1948 and 1958. There is speculation about Cervantes's exact birthday, but it is known that he was born in Alcalá de Henares, some twenty miles from Madrid, in 1547. A certificate of baptism and another one of death are available. There is discussion about his having been a *converso*, that is, a recent convert to Christianity or a member of a recently converted family, although there is a statement dated in 1569 in which he claims *limpieza de sangre e hidalguía*, purity of blood, meaning he was not, at least on paper, a so-called New Christian. Still, suspicions remain, since Jewish converts and their descendants often swore, out of fear, to be *cristianos viejos*. A scattering of other legal documents has survived, among them one detailing a fistfight in which he was involved on the doorstep of his home. But there is little else. No correspondence survives, nor does any other type of record describing his personal or artistic habits.

Although people connect Cervantes with the seventeenth century, in which he published and died, he was in fact a citizen of the sixteenth. He spent most of his adult years living under the rule of Philip II, the king of Castile, whose abuse of power pushed Spain to its disastrous defeat against England in 1588 and whose unstable, almost paranoid views brought along a series of near bankruptcies, the first in 1557, the last in 1596. In spite of its trans-Atlantic military enterprises, which the king consolidated, the nation under him existed in an atmosphere of instability. King Philip III, his successor, named monarch in 1598, was even worse. His diplomatic reputation was mediocre at best. In fact, it is often repeated that Spain's sharp decline took place under the leadership of his corrupt chief, Francisco Gómez de Sandoval, Duque de Lema, during the early years of Philip III's reign, which lasted until 1621.

Cervantes lived at different times in Seville, Valladolid, and Madrid. We know very little about his early years. Perhaps he was a student, maybe even a rowdy one. In 1569, he left Spain for Italy after he wounded a certain Antonio de Segura in a duel. Italy, an artistic and cultural hub in the late sixteenth century, was an obligatory stop for anyone dreaming of making a career in literature. Italian authors play a significant role in *El Quijote*, as in Cervantes's references to Ariosto's *Orlando furioso* and the inspiration he took from Boccaccio's *Decameron*.

In Italy, Cervantes enlisted in the *Infantería de Marina*, the

Spanish Navy Marines, which was stationed in Naples. After a year, he boarded the *Marquesa*, part of a fleet that was controlled by the coalition of the Holy League, which included, along with Spain, the Republic of Venice, the Republic of Genoa, the Duchy of Savoy, and the Knights Hospitaller, who were based in Malta. The mission was to confront expansion of the Ottoman power. In the Battle of Lepanto, on October 7, 1571, he was injured, permanently losing the use of his left arm.

On his way back from Italy, the boat he was sailing on from Naples to Barcelona, the *Sol*, was assaulted by pirates. He and his brother were taken to Algiers, where he was held captive for five years. He tried to escape four times, and on the next attempt he was finally able to flee. *El Quijote* includes a novella, *The Captive's Tale* (First Part, chapters XXXVIII to XLV), possibly inspired by these incidents.

After writing *La Galatea*, to which he promised but never delivered a sequel, Cervantes seemed to have trouble getting his work published. Then, when the First Part of *El Quijote* appeared, the enthusiastic response from readers opened opportunities for him. Between then and the publication of the Second Part a decade later, three other works were printed: a series of mid-size narratives called *Exemplary Novellas* (1613), the satirical poem *Journey to Parnassus* (1614), and his *Comedies*, the latter a volume that included an assortment of *entremeses*.

Thus, Cervantes, in his last phase of life, experienced an outburst of creativity. But nothing he wrote came remotely close to earning the accolades lavished upon *El Quijote*. Indeed, the knight-errant's adventures became so popular that people clamored to read a sequel. As in the case of *La Galatea*, Cervantes promised one but once again was slow in delivering it. Taking advantage of Cervantes's procrastination, another author, using the pseudonymous name Alonso Fernández de Avellaneda, whose full identity remains a secret, came out with a fraudulent Second Part in 1614. (I will discuss this *pseudo-Quijote* in chapter 4, "A Modern Novel.") Cervantes was rightfully incensed. He quickly completed his own Second Part. Fate was generous to him, for he had just enough time to complete and publish it before he died, a few months after its release.

When asked about himself, he glorified his career as a soldier. In one of the most celebrated passages of *El Quijote* (First Part, chapters XXXVII and XXXVIII), about the opposition between arms and letters, Don Quixote, perhaps acting as the author's surrogate, endorses the former in an eloquent speech. "Away with those who assert that letters have the preeminence over arms; I will tell them, whosoever they may be, that they know not what they say," he states. Later on, he adds:

> To attain to eminence in letters costs a man time, watching, hunger, nakedness, headaches, indigestions, and other things of the sort. . . . But for a man to come in the ordinary course of things to be a good soldier costs him all the student suffers, and in an incomparably higher degree, for at every step he runs the risk of losing his life. For what dread of want or poverty that can reach or harass the student can compare with what the soldier feels, who finds himself beleaguered in some stronghold mounting guard in some ravelin or cavalier, knows that the enemy is pushing a mine towards the post where he is stationed, and cannot under any circumstances retire or fly from the imminent danger that threatens him?

In other words, only reluctantly did the most enduring Spanish writer of all time perceive himself as a writer. He probably would have liked to be remembered for his patriotic participation ("the greatest day in history") in Spain's glorious defeat of the Ottomans.

The meager sampling of documents related to Cervantes's life doesn't offer many clues about his looks. No portraits survive, which, again, hasn't stopped people from picturing him in vivid terms. In the collective imagination, the author of *El Quijote* is of average height, slim, and bearded. These qualities are connected to a narrative self-portrait in the prologue to his *Exemplary Novellas*. Nowhere else in his oeuvre is he as candid as he is in this paragraph. He starts by dreaming that the most famous Spanish portraitist of the time, Juan de Jáuregui y Aguilar, had agreed to do his portrait. Then he proceeds to describe his own face. The following quote, rendered into English by Walter K. Kelly in 1952, is from that preface:

> This person whom you see here, with an oval visage, chestnut hair, smooth open forehead, lively eyes, a hooked but well-proportioned nose, & silvery beard that twenty years ago was golden, large moustaches, a small mouth, teeth not much to speak of, for he has but six, in bad condition and worse placed, no two of them corresponding to each other, a figure midway between the two extremes, neither tall nor short, a vivid complexion, rather fair than dark, somewhat stooped in the shoulders, and not very light-footed.

The reference to his dental condition is intriguing. Some find in it evidence that the knight-errant is Cervantes's alter ego, since early on in Don Quixote's exploits (First Part, chapter XVIII) he loses some of his teeth in a fight. Soon thereafter, in an exchange with Sancho in which the pair counts the number of lost teeth, the knight-errant says that "never in my life have I had tooth or grinder drawn, nor has any fallen out or been destroyed by any decay or rheum."

THIS "LIKENESS" OF CERVANTES, as presented in *Exemplary Novellas*, is important because, in the pictorial representations that have been created of the two over time, Cervantes is indeed made to look like Don Quixote and vice versa: they are, in some way, doppelgängers. Needless to say, in a narrative where doubles play an important role, this is no coincidence. In the First Part, chapter I, the knight-errant is described thus: "The age of this gentleman of ours was bordering on fifty; he was of a hardy habit, spare, gaunt-featured, a very early riser and a great sportsman." Cervantes was pushing fifty-eight when the First Part was released, and given his past military adventures, it is easy to imagine him a hardy, early-rising sportsman.

Juan de Jáuregui y Aguilar never produced a portrait of Cervantes, though two forgeries were initially attributed to him. The first one says "Cervantes c. 1600." The second was owned for years by Marqués viudo de Casa Torres. The first portrait of the author, a rather stilted one, depicts him with his mouth closed (i.e., hiding his denture), as is usual in the images of those days, and appeared in the front matter of the French translation of *Exemplary Novellas*, published as *Nouvelles de Michel de Cervantes* in 1705, approximately ninety years after the author's

Cervantes *(c. 1600), attributed to Juan de Jauregui y Aguilar.*

death. The anonymous lithograph presents him sitting at his desk, with a pile of books on the floor. An angelic child floating in the background, an inspiration of genius, offers him a pen, which he intends to hold with his right hand. Cervantes wears a mustache and beard and is dressed in Renaissance attire. But his facial features are dull.

Is this what he looked like? Was his demeanor that of a valiant caballero? A more focused portrayal was produced in 1738 at the London printer J. and R. Tonson, under the auspices of Baron de Carteret. The face has a suspiciously Shakespearean look. Again, Cervantes is sitting at his desk, the right hand writing with a feathered pen, the left hand hidden. Behind him is a small theatrical window in which a knight—it might be Don Quixote himself—makes an appearance. The identity of the artist remains a mystery.

Portrait of Cervantes (1768), engraved by Jacob Folkema.

These two images have been reproduced multiple times throughout the centuries, defining the way we imagine Cervantes. Another engraving, this one done by an artist known as Hulett in London in 1742, portrays Cervantes as a *mestizo*. This may have to do with the fact that Spain, in the eyes of eighteenth-century England, was an awkward, semi-barbaric country close to Africa (known originally as Barbary). But it also prompts the question, to what extent is it accurate to visualize Cervantes through a Caucasian prism? Given the discussion that has taken place over several centuries of his having Jewish blood, and based on his intense interest in things Muslim in his oeuvre, it is possible that the novelist wasn't white. Curiously, there is another portrait by Achille Devéria, done in Paris in 1825, that portrays Cervantes as black.

As mentioned before, Spain in the late sixteenth century was awash in ethnic hullabaloo. *La Convivencia*, a term referring to

*Portrait of Cervantes (1868),
artist unknown.*

the cohabitation in the Iberian Peninsula of Christians, Jews, and Muslims, was coming to an end in 1492, the year of the *Reconquista*, during which the Catholic monarchs Ferdinand and Isabella attempted to unify Spain under a single faith. First they expelled the Jews and then, later the same year, the Arabs. But the previous centuries of cohabitation, brought on by the fall of the Roman Empire and the dissemination of its population across Europe, the Mediterranean Basin, and northern Africa, produced a society marked by racial cross-fertilization, despite the religious tensions and even violence that defined the period.

There is an 1868 portrait, released by the publisher J. B. Lippincott in Philadelphia, its artist unknown, that emphasizes the histrionic, as if Cervantes belonged to a theater troupe. One engraving by C. A. Leslie and Danforth of 1876, published by Porter and Coates, also in Philadelphia, makes him look almost uncomfortable, as if disdaining the attention granted to him. And an oil painting by C. A. Machado, done around 1900, in which Cervantes is holding *El Quijote* with his maimed left arm and has a feather pen in his right hand, casts him in stately terms. Among my favorite portraits of Cervantes is the first pictorial interpretation commissioned by the *Real Academia Española* (*RAE*), the federally funded institution in Madrid charged with safeguarding Spain's cultural heritage. This portrait, by J. del Castillo and Salvador Carmona, based on an image falsely attributed to Alonso del Arco, might be the one most frequently reprinted inside Spain. It was used as the frontispiece in the official *RAE* edition of *Don Quijote de la Mancha* released in 1780. It presents Cervantes as a bearded, fashionable twentieth-century intellectual. The commission came at a time when the Spanish government started to look at Cervantes as an author who could represent the nation's patrimony. (More on this in chapter 6, "*Quijotismo* and *Menardismo*.") That *RAE* edition, by the way, also includes an engraving featuring Don Quixote and Aldonza Lorenzo surrounded by an assortment of characters and motifs, from an African slave to a castle, a lion, and a bonfire of burning books, while an angel descends from heaven with a laurel in hand. Behind all of them is a pedestal in which the title of Cervantes's novel is proudly displayed—*Quixote* spelled with an *x*, not a *j*.

A counterfeited portrait attributed to Diego Velázquez, known as *Velazquez pinx. Dessiné e gravé par Bouvier. Cervantè d'après le tableu original du Cabinet de M. Brière*, appeared in Geneva in 1825. Born in 1599, Velázquez, the baroque court artist, was Cervantes's junior by more than fifty years. When the First Part of *El Quijote* was released, Velázquez was six years old. There is no record of the two having met.

Cervantes (1825), by Charles Bouvier, falsely attributed to Diego Velázquez.

This isn't the only Cervantes portrait falsely attributed to a famous Spanish artist. There are images purportedly painted by El Greco, who was indeed Cervantes's contemporary. Born in Crete, then part of the Republic of Venice, El Greco lived some of his life in Toledo, about forty-five miles from Madrid, where Cervantes died. Another portrait was supposedly made by El Greco's son, Jorge Manuel Theotocópuli.

All these images make Cervantes look like Don Quixote, who, in the First Part, chapter I, is described as "one of those gentlemen that keep a lance in the lance-rack, an old buckler, a lean hack, and a greyhound for coursing." The number of Don Quixote look-alikes and forgeries emphasizes where Cervantes is situated in the Spanish imagination. Fiction begets reality, not the other way around. He is the national author par excellence, whose oeuvre represents the country's idealism as well as its humor.

None of the portraits ever depict Cervantes as anything but an adult. Nor do they present him as a soldier in Lepanto. Or as a captive in Algiers. Instead, they represent a scrapbook of knights. But did Cervantes imagine himself as his knight-errant?

Other sources offer us a hint of how Cervantes perceived himself. In his preface to *El Quijote*, Cervantes describes himself as the owner of a "sterile, ill-tilled wit." (He might have preferred the other epithet awarded him by critics: *el genio lego*, the ignorant genius.) Early in the novel (First Part, chapter VI), we get another perspective when the protagonist, Alonso Quijano, by then already known as Don Quixote, has his personal library inspected by two village censors and the hidalgo's good friends, the priest and the barber. While browsing through the titles, the barber comes across Cervantes's *La Galatea*, which he mentions to the priest. In turn, the priest replies:

> "That Cervantes has been for many years a great friend of mine, and to my knowledge he has had more experience in reverses than in verses. His book has some good invention in it, it presents us with something but brings nothing to a conclusion: we must wait for the Second Part it promises: perhaps with amendment it may succeed in winning the full measure of grace that is now denied it; and in the mean time do you, senor gossip, keep it shut up in your own quarters."

Also in the preface, Cervantes opts to portray himself not as Don Quixote's double, or even as his sibling, but as his father— or better, as his stepfather. He writes in the preface to the First Part:

> Sometimes when a father has an ugly, loutish son, the love he bears him so blindfolds his eyes that he does not see his defects, or, rather, takes them for gifts and charms of mind and body, and talks of them to his friends as wit and grace. I, however—for though I pass for the father, I am but the stepfather to *Don Quixote*—have no desire to go with the current of custom, or to implore thee, dearest reader, almost with tears in my eyes, as others do, to pardon or excuse the defects thou wilt perceive in this child of mine.

Yet while Cervantes's oeuvre at times overshadows him, he doesn't suffer from an "authorship problem" the way Shakespeare does. (Theories abound that the "real" author of Shakespeare's work was someone else, such as Christopher Marlowe; Francis Bacon; William Stanley, the sixth Earl of Derby; Edward de Vere, the seventeenth Earl of Oxford; or even Queen Elizabeth I.) In the Bard's case, the inquiries revolve around a number of issues, among them the mystery of how a provincial actor with a limited education in Stratford-upon-Avon could compose such an erudite, astonishingly diverse body of work. There's no such disassociation with Cervantes. His known journeys through Spain, Italy, northern Africa, and the Mediterranean Sea are present, although tangentially at times, in the pages of *El Quijote*. And the style of the novel is consistent with that of his other works. Plus, in the preface and within his magnum opus there are references to *La Galatea*, Avellaneda, and other aspects of his own career.

In sum, Cervantes might not have left us many clues about his life, but no one believes he was a deceiver, a charlatan, a fraud. What about Don Quixote, though?

2

THE SO-CALLED NORMAL

o same-sex literary pair has ever been as famous, as emulated, or as quoted as Don Quixote and Sancho Panza. One is a nobleman; the other, a villager, a peasant. One is a bachelor; the other, a married man. To the degree that they complement each other, the couple—and a rather odd one—might be taken to represent examples of the "soul mate" theory presented by Plato in the *Symposium* (ca. 385–380 BC), which argues that humans originally had four hands, legs, lungs, and a single head made of two faces, but that Zeus split humans in half, thus creating a person's lifelong longing to find "the other half." The knight-errant and his squire might be seen as one head with two faces, or as the complementing halves of a single soul. One is tall, thin, and bearded. He is an idealist, a dreamer, a full believer in liberty who refuses to accept things as they are, and eager to shape the world according to his own views. The other is short and overweight, down-to-earth as well as materialistic. He pretends to be a family man and is clumsy, unlearned, simpatico, with a tomato nose, a matted beard, and a limited vocabulary, his speech often defaulting into proverbs, folktales, and kitchen knowledge. In his view, things happen in the world for a purpose.

One wears shining armor; the other, plain clothes. One rides a horse, Rocinante; the other, a donkey, Rucio. What kind of relationship do the knight-errant and his squire have? Is it based on economics? On servitude, a feudal legacy? Lionel Trilling, author of *The Liberal Imagination* (1950), believed that in *El Quijote* the real conflict is between social classes, between those who have means to waste and those who don't have enough and live in a constant state of dependency. In somewhat reductionistic fashion, Trilling claims that Cervantes's novel is about how the acquisition of knowledge is achieved through the desire for capital. In other words, it is all about money: the hidalgo has it but doesn't want it; the squire doesn't have it and dreams of it. "Money," Trilling says, is "the great solvent of the solid social fabric of the old society, the great generator of illusion."

Maybe it isn't money but control that is truly at the heart of the novel, controlling the narratives of our own lives. Don Quixote is the master, the owner, the manager of information, who dreams of making reality malleable in order to fit his own views; Sancho is a servant, a subaltern, the receiver of data, who realizes reality is what it is and there's not much anyone can do to change it. Yet as these characters navigate the unsteady geography of Montiel, they become partners and even switch sides. Their conversations are often about interpretation: how to understand something they see or a story they hear. They are constantly arguing, which means control is a game played through language: we use words to make the world fit into the view we have of it.

As a literary pair, Don Quixote and Sancho are legendary, their clones countless in highbrow and popular culture. For starters, the knight-errant is the acknowledged source of inspiration for the rapport between Arthur Conan Doyle's armchair detective Sherlock Holmes and Dr. Watson. Holmes is stuffy, hyper-intellectual, and hard-headed, whereas Watson is pragmatic and flexible. From there on, the echoes in literature are countless. Famous imitations include Ernie and Bert of *Sesame Street*, Dean Martin and Jerry Lewis, Dickens's Mr. Pickwick and Sam Weller in *The Pickwick Papers* (1836), Abbott and Costello, Roberto Bolaño's Arturo Belano and Ulises Lima in *The Savage Detectives* (1998), Laurel and Hardy, Jacques and his master in Diderot's philosophical novel, the dynamic duo Batman and Robin, Vladimir and Estragon in *Waiting for Godot* (1953), Tolkien's Frodo and Sam Gamgee in *The Lord of the Rings* (1954–55), and, in a galaxy far, far away, R2-D2 and C-3PO.

In addition to serving as a model for future literary "odd couples," the relationship between Don Quixote and Sancho is interesting in the influence each character exerts on the other. Salvador de Madariaga, in his book *Don Quixote: An Introductory Essay in Psychology* (1935), talks of two parallel transformations occurring in the novel: the Quixotization of Sancho and the Sanchification of Don Quixote. One becomes the other. John Updike agreed. "It is a stroke of Cervantes' humane genius to see," he stated in a review for the *New Yorker* collected in *More Matter* (1983), "that not only does Don Quixote need

Sancho, but Sancho needs Don Quixote. The earthbound need the release and stimulation of the visionaries, high though the cost be in bruises and embarrassments."

The Quixotization of Sancho is evident in Don Quixote's attempts to correct Sancho's many low-class misbehaviors. In the Second Part, chapter XLIII, the knight-errant gives him a series of recommendations on how to conduct himself once he becomes governor of his own island, Barataria. One of them has to do with having proper manners, in particular not belching in public. "Be temperate in drinking, bearing in mind that wine in excess keeps neither secrets nor promises," the knight says. "Take care, Sancho, not to chew on both sides, and not to eruct in anybody's presence." Manners are an expression of his social status as a hidalgo. He uses them to "civilize" his squire, to make him suitable for power.

Not only does Don Quixote influence Sancho, but Sancho influences Don Quixote as well. At the beginning of the narrative, the knight-errant sees his squire as illiterate and childish. He constantly ridicules the abundance of *dichos*, popular sayings, in Sancho's parlances and, in general, looks down at his capacity to articulate thought. But as the novel progresses, Don Quixote realizes the wisdom in the squire's worldview and, in his own way, begins to shape his own self-image based on what he learns from his companion.

This is done softly, almost invisibly by Cervantes. At one point, after the incident in the Cave of Montesinos, the knight-errant, having attempted to convince his squire that what he saw is true, comes to terms with the fact that he needs concrete, tangible evidence to achieve his goal and doesn't have any. It is at this point that he seems to conclude, to himself, that his subaltern's mind is more methodical, less gullible than his own. And, although he doesn't express it in as many words, Don Quixote distills both admiration and envy toward Sancho's way of handling things.

Yet *El Quijote* isn't only about these two men. It includes a cast of close to eighty important characters. And the couple at its center is really a triangle of sorts, since Don Quixote has an idealized lover, Dulcinea del Toboso, who is really a commoner known as Aldonza Lorenzo. She is often described by him as "my sweet enemy."

Dulcinea's presence in the novel is peculiar. She isn't a character per se since she never really shows up. Don Quixote needs her because every knight-errant has a lady-in-waiting. For instance, at one point (First Part, chapter XIII) he argues that "it is as natural and proper to be in love as to the heavens to have stars: most certainly no history has been seen in which there is to be found a knight-errant without an amour, and for the simple reason that without one he would be held no legitimate knight but a bastard, and one who had gained entrance into the stronghold of the said knighthood, not by the door, but over the wall like a thief and a robber."

His attraction to her isn't sexual but Platonic. This is the essence of courtly love: what matters is not the lover's physical presence but its idealization.

Intriguingly, what the novel doesn't have is an antagonist, a villain, someone with the gravitas of Inspector Javert in *Les Misérables* (1862), Bill Sikes in *Oliver Twist* (1836), Sauron in *The Lord of the Rings*, the Wicked Witch of the West in *The Wizard of Oz* (1900), or Iago in *Othello* (1604). The famous dictum "Every good story has a villain and every villain has a good story" is proved wrong.

Don Quixote makes reference to larger-than-life sorcerers, enchanters, monsters, and ghosts. He frequently tells Sancho about them when he's about to engage in battle. In the knight's eyes, they are the cause of the world's maladies. But none materializes enough to become a full-fledged character. There are, indeed, some minor villains in *El Quijote*. One is Agi Morato in *The Captive's Tale*, the father of Zoraida in Algiers. And there are pseudo-villains, like Samson Carrasco, who is actually a village friend of Alonso Quijano, and Roque Guinart, a Catalan bandit who is rather generous to Don Quixote and Sancho.

Without an antagonist, the novel is turned into a quest, a kind of road narrative. It isn't about enlightenment, since Don Quixote isn't searching for revelation; he already has had that revelation and is ready to act on it. What *El Quijote* is about, therefore, is an exploration of the place where our inner and outer worlds meet. Indeed, Cervantes's narrative moves in two dimensions at once: within the hearts and minds of Don Quixote and Sancho, and through the physical world they actually traverse. They are equally important. Cervantes is meticulous in his realistic depictions. He describes inns and palaces, forests and highways, rivers and mountains. The knight and his squire interact with clerics and the police, attend weddings and funerals, pass through small villages, and arrive in big cities.

Such is the popularity of *El Quijote* that most people's familiarity with the Spanish rural landscape comes as a result of their exposure to the novel, or at least to the endless number of artifacts (movies, paintings, operas, ballets, etc.) derived from it. Not surprisingly, the route of Don Quixote and Sancho is one of the country's most popular tourist attractions today.

In 2007, the *Conseil de l'Europe*, an organization endowed with promoting Europe's cultural heritage, gave its official stamp of approval to an itinerary that starts in the towns of El Toboso, Manzanares, Ossa de Montiel, and Torralba de Cala-trava, then moves to Montiel, especially in the Sierra Morena, where the episode of the windmills takes place. Also set there are the burial of Grisóstomo, the battle with the sheep, the encounter with Cardenio and Dorothea, the episode with Prin-cess Micomicona, and the arrival at the inn where Don Quixote and Sancho meet Lucinda and Don Fernando and hear the cap-tive's story. The journey includes a visit to Toledo as well as to the Cave of Montesinos and reaches as far as Barcelona.

This route has been the stuff of intense curiosity through the ages. The first quixotic effort to pinpoint it dates back to the late eighteenth century, when Tomás López, Spain's royal geographer, published the first detailed map of Don Quixote's travails, which was subsequently endorsed by the *Real Aca-demia Española* as the authentic itinerary in 1780. The fact that the nation's official land surveyor invested his energy in such a task speaks loudly to the status *El Quijote* was already achiev-ing during the European Enlightenment. Cervantes was being turned into a compass, a guide, and, along the way, a source of pride, not only local but also continental.

The wanderings of Don Quixote and Sancho also inspired the itinerary of Azorín, also known as José Martínez Ruiz, the novelist and essayist who died in 1967 at the age of ninety-six and was the foremost Spanish literary critic of his day. For his book *La ruta de don Quijote* (1905), he embarked on a trek that included almost every stop Cervantes mentions. Many of them he found; others he was only able to imagine. That is because, in spite of its realistic bent, *El Quijote* isn't geographically exact. This has been noticed by scores of readers who often find it difficult to connect the dots. Distances aren't realistically conveyed, nor is the time it takes to go from one place to another. Of course, this is a novel, not a tourist guide: Cervantes didn't have an obligation to be accurate. Plenty of locations are invented, such as—most prominently—Barataria, the island of which Sancho ends up becoming governor in the Second Part.

As an imaginary place, Barataria—and, through synecdoche, perhaps all of Quixote's Spain—shares the chemistry of Oz, Middle Earth, Macondo, Yoknapatawpha County, and other nonexistent settings. Still, what makes it peculiar even at that level is that Barataria isn't surrounded by water. It isn't an island but a pseudo-island. Alberto Manguel and Gianni Guadalupi, in *The Dictionary of Imaginary Places* (1980), describe it thus:

> An island somewhere in La Mancha, Spain, in a place whose name does not wish to be remembered, the only island in the world surrounded by land instead of sea.
>
> Barataria is famous for having been governed for a week with honourable rectitude by Sancho Panza, who accompanied the ingenious knight Don Quixote throughout his travels. Sancho Panza abandoned his governorship rather abruptly, after having repelled a fearful enemy invasion, armed only with two wooden tables tied to his waist. (His comments on the island's cuisine were

rather unfavorable—he compared it to a prison diet in time of want.)

Should the traveler visiting Barataria be invited to govern the island, it will be useful to bear in mind some of the advice Don Quixote gave Sancho Panza:

> First fear God; for the fear of God is the beginning of wisdom and a wise man cannot err.
>
> A man should consider what he has been and endeavor to know himself, the most difficult knowledge to acquire.
>
> A man should not be governed by the law of his own whim.
>
> A man should let the tears of the poor find more compassion, but not more justice, than the representations of the rich.
>
> If the scale of justice be at any time not evenly balanced, let it be by the weight of mercy and not by that of a gift.

> It is said that if a governor follows these rules, his days will be long, his fame eternal, his recompense full and his happiness unspeakable.

Barataria might be a caricature—perhaps even a kind of Utopia—reflective of the countries founded by Spanish conquistadors across the Atlantic. When the Second Part of *El Quijote* was published, the Spanish Empire extended from what is the Southwest of the United States today to Patagonia at the tip of South America. In Spain, people envisioned those colonies as a land where quick fortunes were made, courage was tested, and corruption reigned rampant. The indigenous American population was seen as intrinsically inferior, unable to govern itself properly. Not that Spain had stable, dependable rulers, but the colonies were considered an open field where abuse and subjugation prevailed.

In *El Quijote*, the episode about Barataria allows Cervantes to delve into these political issues and fantasies. Sancho, as a peasant, doesn't represent the American mind. Yet his experiment in government must have reminded readers at the time of what was likely to happen when the unprepared—call them the uneducated, even the primitive—take power. The results are likely to be disastrous, not only to them but to civilization in general, for in the end—and therein lies Cervantes's message—rulers are born, not made. Of course, another approach to this section might see it as a political philosophy that endorses a democratic—and maybe even a populist— spirit, represented by the commoner Sancho taking away the power tightly held by monarchists.

Cervantes likely knew as little about the New World as his contemporaries. After his return from Africa, his career as a soldier over, he worked as a tax collector and was accused of mishandling funds. Without a clear future and looking for a clean start, in 1582 he petitioned for an administrative position in New Spain, as Mexico was known at the time. Apparently, for people of his class, going abroad was a way out of difficulties. There is no record of the answer he received, but he never did travel abroad. He applied again in 1590, this time for a position in Colombia, Guatemala, or Bolivia. Once more, he was rejected.

It appears that, for whatever reasons, Cervantes could not escape his life in Spain. Perhaps, like Don Quixote, he escaped into fantasy instead: into a dream of the mind. His characters eat, drink, sleep, bathe, and go about their bodily functions and other daily activities of life, like the rest of us; he feels no need to hide the embarrassing aspects of human behavior. In pairing the idealist knight with a low-class materialist, *El Quijote* turned the fantastical novel of chivalry on its head and paved the way to the kind of psychological realism European literature embraced openheartedly, from Samuel Richardson to Honoré de Balzac, from Ivan Turgenev to Benito Pérez Galdós: the novel not as a distraction from reality but as an embrace of human ordinariness and contradictions; the novel, paraphrasing Haruki Murakami's words, that proves that "what makes us normal is knowing that we're not normal."

3

MADNESS AND METHOD

enry Fielding, the eighteenth-century British novelist and dramatist, who on the title page of his novel *Joseph Andrews* (1742) noted that it is "written in Imitation of the Manner of Cervantes, Author of *Don Quixote*," said, in his play *Rape upon Rape; or, The Justice Caught in His Own Trap and The Coffee-House Politician* (1730), that "the greatest part of mankind labour under one delirium or other, and Don Quixote differed from the rest, not in Madness, but in the species of it."

Everyone is mad; the real question is what kind of madness each of us suffers.

The knight-errant is the most famous madman in literature. But what type of madness does he have? *El Quijote*, of course, doesn't offer a diagnosis per se because the concept of "mental illness" as such is relatively recent, as is the idea of "normal" behavior. Its opposite is deviance, a fixture of the seventeenth century often represented as heresy, witchcraft, and sexual perversion, behaviors often described as demonic.

Since Cervantes left no correspondence, it is impossible to know the degree to which he himself was exposed to deviant behavior, although it is fair to assume that he was familiar with it. Most people lived in Spanish urban centers at the time, and mental illness was a rather public affair. People who didn't conform were described as *herejes*, heretics, and were constantly targeted by the Holy Office of the Inquisition, the most prominent institution representing both religious and political authority, whose mission it was to make the citizenry conform to acceptable norms by publicly punishing those who did otherwise. It wasn't until well into the Enlightenment that attitudes toward the mentally ill became more compassionate, viewing madmen and other deviants as individuals who could be rehabilitated through specific aid.

The earliest psychiatric hospitals—called lunatic asylums—were built in medieval Europe around the thirteenth century. Rather than institutions devoted to offering treatment, though, they were actually custodial wards. It is known that during Cervantes's stay in Seville, there was an active asylum in the city. If he visited it, he would have seen a variety of individuals with diverse diagnoses. It is also documented that his father was a *cirujano barbero*, a surgical barber, which, in the Spanish lingo of the time, meant a surgeon.

El Quijote might be credited for humanizing madness, for making it about the search for freedom. Cervantes isn't attracted to science as a method of understanding the world and to deviant behavior as a feature of that world. But he doesn't dismiss madness as demonic. Nor does he categorize it as irrational. For in truth, Don Quixote is always rational in the way he explains what his motives are and how he wants to embrace them. He takes after Erasmus of Rotterdam, whose book *In Praise of Folly* (1511) was read as a critique of the pious and devout and of the Catholic Church as a corrupt institution.

A taste of Don Quixote's purported madness is offered early on in *El Quijote*, in the First Part, chapter I, when the Narrator, ridiculing the style of novels of chivalry, quotes a far-fetched sentence he claims is typical of these types of noxious books: "*La razón de la sinrazón que a mi razón se hace, de tal manera mi razón enflaquece, que con razón me quejo de vuestra fermosura.*" In Ormsby's translation, the sentence reads: "The reason of the unreason with which my reason is afflicted so weakens my reason that with reason I murmur at your beauty." It can't be sheer coincidence that such a quote, placed in the novel for parodic purposes, also describes the protagonist's own struggle with rationality.

In the late Renaissance, the brain was perceived to have a balance of water: too much of it was noxious; too little was conducive to madness. Robert Burton's *Anatomy of Melancholy* (1621) was released just six years after the publication of the First Part of *El Quijote*. While it didn't reach Spain for a while, the aquatic imagery it proposed is useful for understanding Don Quixote. Burton argued that it is water that allows ideas to connect. He suggested that a baby shedding tears is employing a natural mechanism whereby the brain disposes of its excess of water, thus allowing the right balance for mature intellectual development.

It is said that Alonso Quijano's "brain dried up," as a result of his voracious reading. Here is Samuel Putnam's version (1949):

> In short, our gentleman became so immersed in his reading that he spent whole nights from sundown to sunup and his days from dawn to dusk in poring over his books, until, finally, from so little sleeping and so much reading, his brain dried up and he went completely out of his mind. He had filled his imagination with everything that he had read, with enchantments, knightly encounters, battles, challenges, wounds, with tales of love and its torments, and all sorts of impossible things, and as a result had come to believe that all these fictitious happenings were true; they were more real to him than anything else in the world.

Bizarrely, an English translator like John Ormsby obliterates this section. Ormsby renders it thus (1885):

> In short, his wits being quite gone, he hit upon the strangest notion that every madman in this world hit upon, and that was that he fancied it was right and requisite, as well for the support of his own honour as for the service of his country, that he should make a knight-errant of himself, roaming the world over in full armour and on horseback in quest of adventures.

Not only is the element of water absent, but so is the entire reference to the brain, as well as to reading too much and sleeping too little. The result is rather flat: Don Quixote's wits are gone. The beauty of Cervantes's style is compromised. Worse, the character is simply seen as having lost his mind, whereas in the original, that process is described in loving detail.

Don Quixote's madness has given rise to a full-fledged debate among psychologists, especially those who, in line with Sigmund Freud, are interested in literature as a kind of "dream sequence." At the beginning of the twentieth century, literature faced an entirely new wave of close examination as Freud and his followers, including Carl Gustav Jung, Ernest Jones, and Alfred Adler, began applying a psychoanalytic lens to fictional characters as well as mythological figures.

What resulted were numerous studies suggesting that literary masterpieces, from the Bible to Greek myths, from the folktales and children's stories collected by the German brothers Grimm to Sufism, hold a key to understanding our human desires and impulses. *El Quijote*, too, is part of this canon. There are psychological studies suggesting that *El Quijote* is a study in split personality, referred to in scientific parlance as "dissociative identity disorder," like the half-man, half-beast protagonist in Robert Louis Stevenson's *Strange Case of Dr Jekyll and Mr Hyde* (1886). The range of diagnoses doesn't stop there. Other interpreters believe the knight-errant suffers from bipolar disorder, depression, melancholia, or schizophrenia.

Arguably the most influential of the scientists interested in Cervantes's novel was Sigmund Freud. When he was a young man, Freud discovered Cervantes in Vienna and ended up reflecting psychoanalytically on him, just as he did on biblical characters and classic authors, such as Moses, Sophocles (*Oedipus*), Shakespeare (*Hamlet*), and Goethe (*Faust*). In his late teens and early twenties, while a student at the University of Vienna, Freud was a member of an impromptu club created among friends called *Academia Española*, which centered on Cervantes. They even signed their letters using the names of characters in Cervantes's novella *The Colloquy of the Dogs*, about two talking dogs whose perspective offers a sarcastic portrait of human society. (The novella actually shares characters and motifs with another Cervantes work, *The Deceitful Marriage* [1613].) In their exchange, Freud assumed the role of Cipión, one of the dogs, and his Romanian friend Eduard Silberstein, the role of the other, Berganza. Significantly, one character in *The Colloquy of the Dogs* listens to and advises on the behavior of the other, forming a kind of proto-psychoanalytic relationship between therapist and patient.

Later in life, Freud explained how his infatuation with *El Quijote* persuaded him to learn Spanish, so he could read it in the original and better understand Cervantes's intentions. After studying the novel, he diagnosed the knight-errant as suffering from paranoia, describing him as "the first such recorded case in Western literature." He used the episode of the Cave of Montesinos as an example of Don Quixote's delusions, explaining the knight-errant's experience in the cave as a hallucinatory event.

For Freud, the knight-errant and his squire aren't types but archetypes ingrained in the collective human unconscious. In part because of his fascination, and in part as a result of their own personal connection with this European classic, some of Freud's followers studied Cervantes's novel as well. Jung read the novel to comment on themes like the animus-anima and androgyny. In *Madness and Lust: A Psychoanalytical Approach to Don Quixote* (1983), Carroll B. Johnson, for instance, argued that the entire novel might be read as the story of a man undergoing a midlife crisis who has an incestuous attraction to his niece. In fact, Johnson argued that the entire novel rotates around the protagonist's desire toward women.

The French psychoanalyst and semiotician Michel Foucault maintained in *The Order of Things* (1966) that everything in the book is part of a larger-than-life linguistic code superseding the characters, and that psychology needs to be superseded by linguistics. He thought Don Quixote was connected with this "interplay between resemblance and signs," that he was not "a man given to extravagance, but rather a diligent pilgrim."

In contrast, the Hungarian philosopher György Lukács, who in *The Theory of the Novel* (1920) declared *El Quijote* to be "the first great novel of world literature," explored the psychological dilemma of Don Quixote not from the perspective of psychoanalysis but from that of Marxism. He perceived it as a crossroads where individual dreams and expectations clash with the larger forces of history. Lukács argued that in his madness, the knight-errant confuses what his mind sees with what it projects.

In the end, what makes the exploration of madness in *El Quijote* fascinating is its admirable coherence. Indeed, the plight of the knight-errant is reminiscent of *Hamlet* (1603), in which a depressed, delusional character gets stuck in machinations to the point of inaction. Shakespeare brings his viewers into Hamlet's ordeal by enabling them to follow his philosophical ruminations through lucid soliloquies. But whereas Hamlet, in revenge for his father's death, plots his uncle's demise, ultimately causing his own death, Don Quixote is rather merry about his delusions. He doesn't go inward but outward, hoping to help others through his knightly courage. Different as they are, both types of madmen are disciplined, meticulous, and systematic in the fulfillment of their goals. So much so that, in my view, they are united by one of Shakespeare's play's most famous lines: "Though this be madness, yet there is method in it" (act II, scene 2).

Of course, often in literature, TV, and film, madness is seen as rebellious yet methodical. There is order to it, cause and effect. Looking at it as absolute chaos, as the triumph of disorder, is far more difficult—and it often doesn't make for an appealing artistic representation. Most viewers are frightened by true unruliness. Besides, a work of art in Western civilization is defined as one with an internal logic, especially when it addresses the illogical.

According to German critic Walter Benjamin, Cervantes's novel teaches us "how the spiritual greatness, the boldness, the hopefulness of one of the noblest of men, Don Quixote," appear to others to be devoid of counsel, of roundedness, as if the novel didn't contain "a scintilla of wisdom." And yet it does. Benjamin hits on a valuable dichotomy: madness and wisdom go hand in hand. Lunatics might be seen as wise because, while lacking prudence and judiciousness, their wisdom is delivered in an unadulterated fashion: raw, visceral, and simple. In *El Quijote*, the knight-errant is erudite, even petulant in his rhetorical language, yet his charm is in telling things just as he sees them, not as convention or as others want them to be seen.

To prove Benjamin's point, it is useful to compare Don Quixote to Jesus Christ, something done—as I will show in chapter 6, "*Quijotismo* and *Menardismo*," and chapter 8, "The Ebullient Bunch"—by intellectuals such as Miguel de Unamuno and Fyodor Dostoyevsky. The message delivered by Jesus, as conveyed in the Gospels, is one that might easily be deemed unreasonable: God favors the poor and humble, the devout and unpretentious. Yet Jesus made his case through charisma and eloquence, persuading scores of people to follow him. Was he a lunatic? Perhaps, but the difference between a dreamer and a deranged man is to be found in the steadiness, the reliability of his lesson, against all odds. Jesus was consistent, and so was Don Quixote.

This becomes particularly clear when, after countless adventures, in the climactic moment of *El Quijote* (Second Part, chapter LXXIII), the knight-errant, defeated as he is, returns to his village in La Mancha and, on his deathbed, renounces his actions. It is at this point when Alonso Quijano appears to come back to his senses. But by now all the characters have fallen in love with Don Quixote. Those in attendance beg him not to give up:

> When [they] heard him speak in this way, they had no doubt whatever that some new craze had taken possession of him; and said Samson, "What? Senor Don Quixote! Now that we have intelligence of the lady Dulcinea being disenchanted, are you taking this line; now, just as we are on the point of becoming shepherds, to pass our lives singing, like princes, are you thinking of turning

hermit? Hush, for heaven's sake, be rational and let's have no more nonsense."

Everyone wants Don Quixote not to revert to his previous persona of Alonso Quijano. Everyone wants him to go on inhabiting his dream, which by that point has also become theirs. Isn't this proof that the knight-errant is not mad?

4

A MODERN NOVEL

he act of burning books is not new. It is well known that the first emperor of China, Shih Huang Ti, who ordered the building of the Great Wall of China, also commanded the destruction of all books that mentioned the past prior to his arrival. The destruction of books was a way for the emperor to erase memory and rewrite history. More than twenty centuries later, on the night of November 9, 1938, known as *Kristallnacht*, the Nazi government attacked Jews and their businesses throughout Germany and parts of Austria. Bonfires were made to destroy Jewish books.

Likewise, during the reign of Philip II in Spain, the Holy Office of the Inquisition began its infamous *Index of Censored Books* in 1551. The Catholic Church started keeping the list, meant to be a statement of prohibition against foreign ideas connected with the Reformation in England and with incipient manifestations of the Enlightenment. Among the forbidden books were *In Praise of Folly* by Erasmus and *The Lazarillo de Tormes*, a classic Spanish novella about the misfortunes of a *pícaro*, a young rogue, that began to circulate probably around 1552 but whose surviving first editions date to 1554. Reading those books meant being subjected to punishment. Ironically, that punishment made the books all the more alluring.

Such are the events that no doubt inspired the scene in *El Quijote*'s First Part, chapter VI, in which Alonso Quijano's books are burned. In it, the priest and the barber enter Alonso Quijano's library while Don Quixote is asleep, and comment on several of the volumes they find in it. Their objective is twofold: to diagnose the knight-errant's madness based on the books found in his alter ego's library; and to cleanse that library, eliminating the noxious books, in order to bring back Quijano, that is, to cure him. The priest and the barber condemn the books by throwing them out the window, where they are set on fire by Quijano's niece. The scene is obviously about intolerance during Cervantes's time. Yet it is humorous, almost endearing.

In the setting of seventeenth-century Spain, the size and the scope of Quijano's library, as described in *El Quijote*, is rather extraordinary. In the First Part, chapter XXIV, the Narrator says it contains a hundred books, although later Don Quixote himself claims to have some three hundred. Either way, the amount suggests not only a committed reader but also a devoted collector.

Only twenty-nine books are mentioned by title, though. Obviously, the barber and the priest come across several novels of chivalry, including *Amadis of Gaul*, *Espejo de caballerías*, *Palm-*

erín de Inglaterra, Belianís de Grecia, and Tirant lo Blanc. These volumes are saved because the barber and the priest have a positive opinion of them, but other chivalry titles are thrown to their destruction. The two censors also come across pastoral romances and epic poetry, of which eleven books are spared and five are burned.

At one point, of course, the priest and the barber find Cervantes's own La Galatea, about which they don't have good things to say, although they find its author promising and, thus, decide to save the book. Aside from being a charming moment of self-reflection, the scene showcases the extent to which El Quijote as a whole is also about literary criticism: it not only parodies novels of chivalry but also meditates on the redemptive value of fine writing in general.

Censorship, in short, is portrayed as a double-edged sword. It is a sign of intolerance, of repression. Yet, ironically, the whole affair has a positive effect, for the priest and the barber, in selecting what is worthy from what is trash, become unlikely agents of change. Their action suggests that censorship is the mother of metaphor, that to write in an atmosphere of fear means to give the imagination an alternative way out.

Though El Quijote, in part because of this scene, but also in general as a result of its protagonist's indefatigable spirit to fight all forms of oppression, has become an exemplar against censorship, there is no indication that the early seventeenth century saw the novel as condemning censorship. No actual copies were ever burned. Like all writers of his time, Cervantes submitted his manuscript to a censoring committee. At the opening, he included a dedication to his benefactor, the Duke of Béjar. He used the occasion to offer, in passing, a backhanded critique of censors: they, he argues, *"continiéndose en los límites de su ignorancia, suelen condenar con más rigor y menos justicia los trabajos ajenos,"* containing themselves to the limits of their ignorance, often condemn other people's work with more rigor and less justice. Their method isn't about fairness but about allegiance to the ideology in power.

Even as the Catholic Church demonstrated its power, opposing forces had begun to emphasize individualism and reject the ubiquity of the church. A slew of influential late Renaissance works proved that a movement toward modernity was under way: Erasmus of Rotterdam's *In Praise of Folly* (1511), Michel de Montaigne's personal *Essays* (1580), Descartes's *Discourse on the Method* (1637), Spinoza's *Tractatus Theologico-Politicus* (1677), and the Shakespearean canon. In equal measure, the French intellectuals who surrounded the making of *Encyclopédie* pointed to an alternative to the static, religion-driven universe in which the postponement of reward was based on an accepted vision of the afterlife. Erasmus, a Dutch humanist and Catholic priest, as well as a friend of Thomas More, used the character of Folly to attack pious priests and celebrate madness. Descartes's dictum *cogito ergo sum*—I think, therefore I am—placed the mind, the act—and the art—of thinking, at the center of human existence. Montaigne, through his *que sais-je?*—who am I?—looked at the self as the sole motor in human life. Spinoza critiqued the Bible as a bunch of children's stories and suggested that God is the natural workings of the universe itself. Shakespeare looked at humans as fragile, ambitious, and driven by passion. And the French encyclopedists sought to codify the vastness of human knowledge, to tame it, to make it purposeful. What they all have in common is the angst that results from finding out that every person is nurtured by inner desires, and those desires—not the Almighty—are a driving force of human events. *Angst* is synonymous with *doubt, confusion,* and *uncertainty.* In the case of Cervantes, the novel as a literary genre could be a vehicle to fully express this predicament.

Premodern literary artifacts—including the novels of chivalry—were about heroes doing gallant deeds, exhibiting signs of courage, even superhuman qualities. Odysseus in *The Odyssey*, for instance, is less a person than a symbol, a representation of human will. Equally, the characters in *The Divine Comedy* are archetypes. Even Dante himself is an emblem of the spiritual seeker. And in Chaucer's *Canterbury Tales*, the assortment of Londoners creates a parade of stereotypes. In Spain, there is Fernando de Rojas's *Celestina* (1499), about a procuress of an illicit love affair, and the anonymous *Lazarillo of Tormes* (1554), about a boy who serves various masters, among other medieval examples.

None of these works have the keen attribute of the modern work of literature, in which a character undergoes an inner transformation from the beginning to the end of the narrative. Don Quixote is mentally and physically in one place at the beginning and in another place at the end, and in the interim he undergoes a gamut of radical changes. These changes entail learning about his own frailties and, consequently, realizing he isn't as stolid, as resistant as he originally thought. As a result, he loses his idealism. The quintessential modern novel is the *bildungsroman*, or coming-of-age plot, with growing up being human life's most universal, relatable form of inner and outer change. Indeed, change is what modernity is about.

Modern literature also cares about being credible, reliable, even "authentic," all the while aware of being an invention. Indeed, what Cervantes strives for in his depiction of Don Quixote and Sancho is verisimilitude. This aspect is studied with acumen by the German philologist Erich Auerbach in *Mimesis: The Representation of Reality in Western Literature* (1953), written in Turkey in 1935 while he was in exile because of the Nazi takeover in Germany. Chapter 14, called "The Enchanted Dulcinea," looks at Don Quixote's love for his lady. Auerbach meditates on the way fact and fiction, dreams and reality are juxtaposed in the novel. Aldonza Lorenzo has no clue that the knight-errant and his squire have turned her into an object of adoration. As a villager concerned with her own affairs, she rejects the knight's passes whenever they take place. But Don Quixote is undeterred. For him she is the essence of authenticity. And he pursues her, his true love, without end. Her complete lack of affectation becomes a complement to his intellectual follies. Auerbach writes:

> The theme of a mad country gentleman who undertakes to revive knight-errantry gave Cervantes an opportunity to present the world as play in that spirit of multiple, perspective, non-judging, and even non-questioning neutrality which is a brave form of wisdom.

That rare form of wisdom, for Auerbach, is expressed in *El Quijote* in another dimension: its attempt to depict reality—especially, in my view, the reality of the human body—as accurately as possible.

This surely isn't a dirty novel. Eschatology is kept in check.

Sex is nonexistent. No reference is given to erogenous zones. Yet *El Quijote* traffics in reliability: for better or worse, its characters feel real, like the rest of us. They stumble, become disoriented, make foolish mistakes. In short, they are imperfect. They even pass gas, as Cervantes tells us at hilarious length in chapter XX of the First Part. The episode is worth quoting in full. The knight and his squire are sitting around a campfire:

> Just then, whether it was the cold of the morning that was now approaching, or that he had eaten something laxative at supper, or that it was only natural (as is most likely), Sancho felt a desire to do what no one could do for him; but so great was the fear that had penetrated his heart, he dared not separate himself from his master by as much as the black of his nail; to escape doing what he wanted was, however, also impossible; so what he did for peace's sake was to remove his right hand, which held the back of the saddle, and with it to untie gently and silently the running string which alone held up his breeches, so that on loosening it they at once fell down round his feet like fetters; he then raised his shirt as well as he could and bared his hind quarters, no slim ones. But, this accomplished, which he fancied was all he had to do to get out of this terrible strait and embarrassment, another still greater difficulty presented itself, for it seemed to him impossible to relieve himself without making some noise, and he ground his teeth and squeezed his shoulders together, holding his breath as much as he could; but in spite of his precautions he was unlucky enough after

all to make a little noise, very different from that which was causing him so much fear.

Don Quixote, hearing it, said, "What noise is that, Sancho?"

"I don't know, senor," said he; "it must be something new, for adventures and misadventures never begin with a trifle." Once more he tried his luck, and succeeded so well, that without any further noise or disturbance he found himself relieved of the burden that had given him so much discomfort. But as Don Quixote's sense of smell was as acute as his hearing, and as Sancho was so closely linked with him that the fumes rose almost in a straight line, it could not be but that some should reach his nose, and as soon as they did he came to its relief by compressing it between his fingers, saying in a rather snuffing tone, "Sancho, it strikes me thou art in great fear."

"I am," answered Sancho; "but how does your worship perceive it now more than ever?"

"Because just now thou smellest stronger than ever, and not of ambergris," answered Don Quixote.

"Very likely," said Sancho, "but that's not my fault, but your worship's, for leading me about at unseasonable hours and at such unwonted paces."

Earlier writers shared this delight in earthy humor for sure; examples abound in the works of Rabelais, Boccaccio, Chaucer, and others. But the larger context of the humor differs. Significantly, while the Catholic Church plays an integral role in the society of Don Quixote and Sancho, Cervantes's worldview is, for all intents and purposes, nonreligious. That is, his protagonist, the knight, doesn't seek salvation through doctrinal faith. Indeed, *El Quijote* is arguably the first work of fiction in which living people debate their own fate and battle their own demons.

Another way that *El Quijote* differs dramatically from its premodern predecessors is in its self-referentiality and blurring of the boundaries between fiction and reality. Self-referentiality was a fixture of the Spanish Golden Age. The literature of this period, aside from works by Lope de Vega, included those of Francisco de Quevedo, Luis de Góngora, Pedro Calderón de la Barca, and the Mexican nun Sor Juana Inés de la Cruz, all of whom were fascinated with labyrinths, mirrors, and a style that called attention to itself (the Argentine man of letters Leopoldo Lugones said that "*el estilo es la debilidad de Cervantes*," style is Cervantes's weakness), to the point of becoming an artifice. That style, which also manifested itself in music, architecture, and painting, isn't easy to define. Jorge Luis Borges, another Argentine *hombre de letras*, tried to do it in the prologue to his collection of essays *Discusión* (1938): "I should define the baroque as that style which deliberately exhausts (or tries to exhaust) all its own possibilities and which borders on its own parody."

Among the best examples of that style are Diego Velázquez's *Las Meninas* (1656), a painting preoccupied with reflections, and Lope de Vega's "*Soneto de repente*," which is a sonnet about writing a sonnet. *El Quijote*, too, is a book about books, a book about itself, a book about the limits of literature. Its overall structure is that of reflections reflecting reflections. Harry Levin, a Harvard scholar (I will discuss his work in chapter 9, "America's Exceptionalism"), said that "when Pascal observed

that when true eloquence makes fun of eloquence, he suc-
cinctly formulated the principle that could look to Cervantes
as its recent and striking exemplar." Levin described that
principle as "looking at life as a performance." Lionel Trilling
agreed: "Cervantes sets for the novel the problem of appearance and reality."

It is hard to overstate what a huge leap it was for art to start
referencing itself and thereby to blur its boundaries with reality. Carlos Fuentes and Milan Kundera credit *El Quijote* with
opening up a postmodern viewpoint that paved the way to
future self-referential novels such as Laurence Sterne's *Tristram Shandy* (1759) and philosophical works like Diderot's
Jacques the Fatalist (1796).

THE GROUNDBREAKING PREOCCUPATION with appearance
and reality of Cervantes's novel is clear from the moment Alonso
Quijano acts the role of Don Quixote. From there on, the game
is constant. In the Second Part, several characters are said to be
readers of the First Part. They have an exchange with the knight-
errant and his squire about this—they are aware of themselves as
literary characters. They complain about being misrepresented.
They know they have been, in Spanish, *literalizados*, turned into
literature. This happens in chapter III, as Don Quixote talks with
Samson Carrasco:

> Don Quixote made him rise, and said, "So, then, it is true
> that there is a history of me, and that it was a Moor and a
> sage who wrote it?"

"So true is it, senor," said Samson, "that my belief is there are more than twelve thousand volumes of the said history in print this very day. Only ask Portugal, Barcelona, and Valencia, where they have been printed, and moreover there is a report that it is being printed at Antwerp, and I am persuaded there will not be a country or language in which there will not be a translation of it."

"One of the things," here observed Don Quixote, "that ought to give most pleasure to a virtuous and eminent man is to find himself in his lifetime in print and in type, familiar in people's mouths with a good name; I say with a good name, for if it be the opposite, then there is no death to be compared to it."

"If it goes by good name and fame," said the bachelor, "your worship alone bears away the palm from all the knights-errant; for the Moor in his own language, and the Christian in his, have taken care to set before us your gallantry, your high courage in encountering dangers, your fortitude in adversity, your patience under misfortunes as well as wounds, the purity and continence of the platonic loves of your worship and my lady Dona Dulcinea del Toboso—"

"I never heard my lady Dulcinea called Dona," observed Sancho here; "nothing more than the lady Dulcinea del Toboso; so here already the history is wrong."

"That is not an objection of any importance," replied Carrasco.

"Certainly not," said Don Quixote; "but tell me, senor bachelor, what deeds of mine are they that are made most of in this history?"

"On that point," replied the bachelor, "opinions differ, as tastes do; some swear by the adventure of the windmills that your worship took to be Briareuses and giants; others by that of the fulling mills; one cries up the description of the two armies that afterwards took the appearance of two droves of sheep; another that of the dead body on its way to be buried at Segovia; a third says the liberation of the galley slaves is the best of all, and a fourth that nothing comes up to the affair with the Benedictine giants, and the battle with the valiant Biscayan."

"Tell me, senor bachelor," said Sancho at this point, "does the adventure with the Yanguesans come in, when our good Rocinante went hankering after dainties?"

"The sage has left nothing in the ink-bottle," replied Samson; "he tells all and sets down everything, even to the capers that worthy Sancho cut in the blanket."

"I cut no capers in the blanket," returned Sancho; "in the air I did, and more of them than I liked."

"There is no human history in the world, I suppose," said Don Quixote, "that has not its ups and downs, but more than others such as deal with chivalry, for they can never be entirely made up of prosperous adventures."

Then there is the section, in the Second Part, chapter XXVI, in which Don Quixote and Sancho come across a puppet show orchestrated by Master Pedro, who the reader eventually finds out is also the character of Ginés de Pasamonte. The story told through the puppets begins in France and takes place when Zaragoza (known in the story as Sansueña) was under Moorish rule. It pertains to the rescue of Melisendra, the alleged daughter of Charlemagne who is held captive by the Moors in the tower of the city's castle. The theme, then, has strong religious as well as nationalistic undertones: it is about Catholic Spain fighting the infidels in order to free the country from oppression.

Melisendra's husband, Don Gaiferos, crosses the Pyrenees to rescue her. As they escape, the city is in turmoil, with the bells in the minarets sounding the alarm. Don Quixote, while watching the show, occasionally interrupts with complaints about accuracy and other qualms. As the Moors pursue the Catholic lovers, the knight-errant becomes agitated. Using chivalric language, he tells the puppets to stop and then uses his sword to destroy the set and the puppets as Master Pedro watches in desperation.

The Spanish philosopher José Ortega y Gasset, author of *Meditations on Quixote* (1914) and *The Revolt of the Masses* (1930), found this section intriguing. "The frame of the puppet show," he argued, "which Master Pedro goes around presenting, is the dividing line between two continents of the mind." He adds, "The puppet show itself represents the world of adventure. Outside is an audience, perhaps unsophisticated in its capacity to reflect on the puppet performance. And in between is a deranged man who believes he is a knight-errant. A puppet show is inside a puppet show that is inside a puppet show."

Another episode that takes place at the Cave of Montesinos (Second Part, chapters XXII and XXIII) also erodes the boundaries between life and stage. The actual cave exists in La Mancha in the province of Ciudad Real, near the town of Ossa de Montiel. Entering alone, Don Quixote purportedly undergoes a mystical experience. When he comes out, he tells Sancho of his adventures, which appear to have taken place over several days. He describes wonder after wonder and even suggests having come across Dulcinea herself.

> "I recognized her," said Don Quixote, "by her wearing the same garments she wore when thou didst point her out to me. I spoke to her, but she did not utter a word in reply; on the contrary, she turned her back on me and took to flight, at such a pace that crossbow bolt could not have overtaken her."

But the squire tells him he has been in the cave for only a few hours. This crucial episode is a decisive moment, for the squire finally contests Don Quixote's authority, doubting the veracity of his words, creating a new balance of power between them:

> "O blessed God!" exclaimed Sancho aloud at this, "is it possible that such things can be in the world, and that enchanters and enchantments can have such power in it as to have changed my master's right senses into a craze so full of absurdity! O senor, senor, for God's sake, consider yourself, have a care for your honour, and give no credit to this silly stuff that has left you scant and short of wits."
> "Thou talkest in this way because thou lovest me, Sancho," said Don Quixote; "and not being experienced in the things of the world, everything that has some difficulty about it seems to thee impossible; but time will pass, as I said before, and I will tell thee some of the things I saw down there which will make thee believe what I have

related now, the truth of which admits of neither reply nor question."

What is meant to have actually happened in the Cave of Montesinos has generated much discussion among scholars. Salvador de Madariaga argued that it "comes in as a sort of 'harmonic' of the whole book, an illusion within the illusion, like the seed within the fruit. In it Don Quixote touches the fringes of reality and appears to us partly in the sunshine of sound sense, partly in the shadow of madness."

This argument points to Don Quixote's perspective: Is the reader supposed to even believe him as the conveyer of facts in the novel? Or is what he says always questionable? The reader ponders another dimension to the novel: the trust extended, or not, to the narrator of the story.

Actually, *El Quijote* doesn't have one narrator but at least three. First is the omniscient, first-person Narrator (spelled here, though not in the novel, with a capital *N*, in order to identify him as a specific individual), whose name remains unmentioned; second, an Arab historian called Cide Hamete Benengeli; and third, the translator who makes that historian's work available in Spanish. Often their interplay is contradictory. Added to these layers is an oral tradition from which the original storyline about Alonso Quijana appears to emerge.

The oral component is present from the beginning. In the First Part, chapter I, the Narrator says other versions of the life and times of Alonso Quijano are available in La Mancha but that incongruences reign among them. (There is speculation among literary historians that Cervantes might have based the character of Don Quixote on a person by the name of Domingo Pacheco, who lived in the town of Argamasilla de Alba, in the province of Ciudad Real.) In the face of such ambiguity, the Narrator, like an anthropologist, assumes an authoritative position, selecting the oral version that is most acceptable, or at least the one he is most comfortable with. He does so not only throughout the First Part but in the Second Part as well. Who this narrator is and what relationship he had with Cervantes as an author are never explained.

Then comes the Arab historian. In the First Part, chapter IX, the Narrator tells of coming across an old manuscript when, in Toledo, a boy "came up to sell some pamphlets and old papers to a silk mercer." The manuscript was called "History of Don Quixote of La Mancha, written by Cide Hamete Benengeli, an Arab Historian." There, the Narrator asks *un morisco aljamiado*, a Muslim convert, to prepare a quick translation, which is what we read as the majority of the novel.

In the tense atmosphere of ethnic relations that prevailed in Spain in the seventeenth century, the idea of making an Arab the true author of the knight-errant's story is astounding. Muslims in Cervantes's time were held in little regard. For the Narrator to suggest that a *morisco* knows more about Don Quixote than anyone else is a slap in the face to the nation's Christian mores.

Occasionally, the Narrator questions the veracity of the story by suggesting that the translator has done a poor job or by implying that Arabs, even Arab historians, cannot be trusted. For instance, at the beginning of the Second Part, chapter XLIV, the Narrator discusses some liberties the translator took with the "original":

It is stated, they say, in the true original of this history, that when Cide Hamete came to write this chapter, his interpreter did not translate it as he wrote it—that is, as a kind of complaint the Moor made against himself for having taken in hand a story so dry and of so little variety as this of Don Quixote, for he found himself forced to speak perpetually of him and Sancho, without venturing to indulge in digressions and episodes more serious and more interesting. He said, too, that to go on, mind, hand, pen always restricted to writing upon one single subject, and speaking through the mouths of a few characters, was intolerable drudgery, the result of which was never equal to the author's labour, and that to avoid this he had in the First Part availed himself of the device of novels, like "The Ill-advised Curiosity," and "The Captive Captain," which stand, as it were, apart from the story.

In short, *El Quijote* is the tale of a found palimpsest. From here on, Benengeli is described as "the true author," whereas the Narrator becomes a commentator on the original story delivered by the *historiador arábigo*, as translated by the *morisco aljamiado*. It is important to note that the name Cide Hamete Benengeli is itself a parody: *Cide* is Arabic for *señor* (as in El Cid, The Señor) and *Benengeli* is a variation on the word *berenjena*, eggplant, a favorite ingredient in Middle Eastern cuisine.

The fictional palimpsest spanned a real one (or at least an attempt at a real one): just as Cide Hamete's manuscript achieved an afterlife in the hands of first a translator and then a narrator within the novel, *El Quijote* itself took on new life in another author's hands when a bogus follow-up suddenly materialized in 1614—*Segunda parte del ingenioso hidalgo don Quijote de la Mancha*, authored by one Alonso Fernández de Avellaneda—before Cervantes even completed his own second part. Avellaneda's book is commonly known as "the false *Quijote*" as well as the *"pseudo-Quijote."* I prefer the latter.

In the tradition of chivalry literature, novels such as *Felixmante de Hircania* and *Palmerin de Inglaterra* gave place to new installments, sometimes written by other hands and in different languages. Certainly aware of this trait, Cervantes, at the end of the First Part, promises a sequel. Perhaps he made the promise because he wanted to attract readers to his other forthcoming works. But life interfered and none materialized for a decade. Audiences were eager, and Avellaneda capitalized on the public hunger.

Avellana in Spanish means "hazelnut"; *Avellanado*, "hazel wood." Little is known about this author, although, again, as in the case of the controversy surrounding Shakespeare's authorship, there have been all sorts of "unveilings" of potential perpetrators. One possibility is that Avellaneda was Jerónimo de Pasamonte, on whom Cervantes appears to have modeled the character of Ginés de Pasamonte (also known as Master Pedro). Another possibility is Pedro Liñán de Riaza, a popular novelist at the time who was a friend of both Cervantes and Lope de Vega. Since Liñán died in 1607, the argument is made that some of Lope's friends, including Pasamonte, as well as Baltasar Elisio de Medinilla, Lupercio Leonardo de Argensola, and Cristóbal Suárez de Figueroa, contributed to the completion of the work.

Ironically, what we do know about Avellaneda comes from the *pseudo-Quijote* and from *El Quijote* itself. In the Second Part of *El Quijote* written by Cervantes, the Narrator describes Avellaneda as an Aragonese from the town of Tordesillas, a "great, coarse, ill-trimmed ostrich" with a "frozen wit." It's clear he is aware of Spanish literary circles and that he might have been an admirer of Lope de Vega, since in the *pseudo-Quijote* Avellaneda takes Cervantes to task for having limited talents, being one-handed, and envying Lope.

It wasn't uncommon in Cervantes's day for unofficial sequels of literary works to appear. *The Lazarillo of Tormes*, for instance, inspired not one but two. Other popular books also fostered follow-ups, which in general were derivative and, for the most part, poorly written. That is the case with Avellaneda's work. Its style is trite and uninspired, its storyline confusing, its character development unripe. This, in short, is the product of a lousy writer. Today, he is seen as a Judas figure: a traitor, an impostor. However, since there was no copyright law in Cervantes's time, Avellaneda was not legally forbidden to co-opt another person's creations. But he was certainly morally wrong. Or was he? Plagiarism is directly linked to the concept of private intellectual property. Yet during the Renaissance, such a concept had little appeal. Authors often stole ideas, characters, and entire plots from their admired predecessors as a way to pay tribute to them, to declare them role models.

But perhaps here there is a *truco cervantino*, a literary trick. Could it be that Cervantes himself was Avellaneda? In other words, what if Avellaneda never existed—what if the real author of *El Quijote* also wrote the lousy *pseudo-Quijote*? It's an implausible, absurd, far-fetched idea, yet one that is undoubtedly entertaining. Since posterity knows little about this "pretended" author, it is easy to speculate. What if Avellaneda is a device, and his apocryphal novel Cervantes's own effort to get his novelistic juices flowing? After all, Cervantes had already created another pretend author: the Arab historian Cide Hamete Benengeli. Couldn't he simply multiply the effort by two?

The problem with this theory is that stylistic analysis of Avellaneda's sequel does not reveal similar traits—for example, the same syntactical database, or the emphatic use of grammatical signs. Even the idea that Lope's friends co-wrote it is implausible because the work is replete with an Aragonese jargon only a native would be able to employ freely. Yet Cervantes hasn't been put through the same scrutiny that Shakespeare has. Digital examination of Shakespeare's works has enabled us to understand how his use of language changed over time, what percentage of his own writing is present in his collaborations with other playwrights, and what kind of continuity there is between the syntax in the sonnets *Venus and Adonis* and *The Rape of Lucrece* and later plays like *Macbeth* (1606) and *The Tempest* (1610–11). We don't have digital data to compare the First and the Second Part of *El Quijote* written by Cervantes, let alone to see any unlikely similarities between *El Quijote* and the *pseudo-Quijote*.

El Quijote uses the Avellaneda impostureship to test its own limits. Frequently in the Second Part, Don Quixote and Sancho are aware of their own existence as literary characters. They decry their cheapening portraits in the pseudo–Second Part, as when, in the Second Part, chapter LXII, Don Quixote and Sancho, in a print shop in Barcelona, come across a book called

"'The Second Part of the Ingenious Gentleman Don Quixote of La Mancha,' by one of Tordesillas."

"I have heard of this book already," said Don Quixote, "and verily and on my conscience I thought it had been by this time burned to ashes as a meddlesome intruder. . . . [F]or fictions have the more merit and charm about them the more nearly they approach the truth or what looks like it; and true stories, the truer they are the better they are;" and so saying he walked out of the printing office with a certain amount of displeasure in his looks.

Don Quixote therefore suggests that fiction is true when it is also original and authentic. Likewise, Cervantes attacks his rival author at every turn, accusing him of dishonesty and, worse, of having a second-rate talent:

For me alone was Don Quixote born, and I for him; it was his to act, mine to write; we two together make but one, notwithstanding and in spite of that pretended Tordesillesque writer who has ventured or would venture with his great, coarse, ill-trimmed ostrich quill to write the achievements of my valiant knight;—no burden for his shoulders, nor subject for his frozen wit: whom, if perchance thou shouldst come to know him, thou shalt warn to leave at rest where they lie the weary mouldering bones of Don Quixote, and not to attempt to carry him off.

These comments make the novel anxious, impatient with itself. They also explore issues of authenticity as well as control. What is real and what is art? To what extent is our life a performance?

El Quijote becomes a hall of mirrors. Is its Narrator truly at the helm? And if Cide Hamete Benengeli is actually the real author, why can't Avellaneda also be "a real second author"? In the end, the novel is a series of reflections that question modernity—its limits, its implications—while also endorsing it as a way of life.

5

THE CONJUROR OF WORDS

l Quijote has a total of 2,059,005 letters and 381,104 words. There are some 4,160 end-of-sentence periods, 4,040 end-of-paragraph periods, 40,165 commas, 4,800 semicolons, 20,050 colons, 960 question marks, and 690 exclamation marks. The latter is significant: while the exclamation mark is pervasive in our electronic age, particularly on Twitter (!!!), during the Renaissance it was modestly employed. Its role was to convey wonder, not to exaggerate it. Cervantes might be considered an early champion of it.

In the most authoritative edition of the novel, known in Spanish as *Don Quijote de la Mancha*, edited by Francisco Rico in 1998 and issued under the aegis of Instituto Cervantes, the most frequently used word is *que* (meaning "what" or "who," used to introduce subordinate clauses), featured as either a preposition or a conjunction. It shows up 20,617 times; that is, it constitutes 5.41 percent of the complete text.

It is emblematic that the word *Quijote* is present 2,174 times in the novel, with the word *Sancho* coming closely behind with 2,147 instances, and *Dulcinea* lagging behind at 282. For a novel published in an age of religious fanaticism, it is somewhat surprising that the word *dios*, Spanish for "God," shows up only 516 times. The word *verdad*, truth, appears nearly as often, 431 times.

And here's the essential number: *El Quijote* has a total of 22,939 different words. This number represents the author's verbal reservoir in his magnum opus. Shakespeare, in contrast, used slightly more: a total of 29,066 different English words in the sum of his plays.

Cervantes's most lasting contribution is the depth and complexity of his language. A conjuror of words, he pushed Spanish beyond its boundaries. He didn't revolutionize language like Shakespeare did—the Bard coined close to 1,700 new words that have become common over time, such as *academe, amazement, champion, discontent, gossip, hurried, fashionable, laughable, majestic, pedant, unreal*, and *zany*. In that sense, Cervantes was rather conventional. His innovation is found in his linguistic plasticity, in the way he uses standard words to create a multifarious reality.

Through a novel that has magically survived its own context, Cervantes's syntax has become the default standard style in Spanish. *Cervantistas* have spilled large amounts of ink explaining, in great detail, how his language functions, what his lexical preferences are, his ticks, his mistakes, the influences he got from previous Spanish authors. I won't purport to replicate, or even to survey, those scholarly studies in these pages. However, there is consensus that Cervantes's capacity to summon the Spain of the seventeenth century in all its complexity, his talent to understand the tension between our inner reality and the world that surrounds us, his power to use language to scrutinize the complexity of human nature—all are done through a spirited, improvisational style that never feels caged.

Writing at the crest of the Enlightenment, a time when there was a clear distinction between highbrow, sophisticated scholarly language (still embodied in Latin although dwindling in favor of the vernacular) and the parlance of the people, he succeeded in reflecting this cultural divide in the linguistic *paso doble*, the dialogue between Don Quixote and Sancho, a nobleman and a villager, as well as through the parlance of other socially diverse characters, from a priest to a barber, from a hostel owner to a duke and a duchess. His use of the particular *lengua romance* called *castellano*, Castilian, also known as *español*, Spanish, offered a cornucopia of possibilities.

To understand those possibilities, it is crucial to appreciate the linguistic forces that affected Cervantes. The Spanish language, a bit more than a century before Cervantes used it as a conduit in *El Quijote*, was a witness to Spain's consolidation as a nation-state. This consolidation came about when the *indeseables* (Jews and Arabs) were pushed out and while colonies (including those in America) were being incorporated into the empire. The creation of the first Spanish-language press in Valencia in 1474 and its subsequent expansion also contributed to the cornucopia of artistic, political, and economic possibilities that would flourish during the Spanish Golden Age.

In the early seventeenth century, however, the Spanish Empire, perhaps the richest on the globe, was profoundly fractured, its economy in shambles. Tax evasion ran rampant. Corruption prevailed. Political cronyism was the law of the land.

The Crown depended on the wealth imported from the American colonies to pay for its budget deficit.

This resulted in a dramatic class divide. Whereas capitalism had taken hold in different European nations, among them Germany, France, and Italy, where an emergent bourgeoisie was already assuming a leading role, Spain remained stuck in a feudal mentality. Don Quixote's stilted language is that of a lowly nobleman, while his squire, Sancho Panza, peppers his parlance with *dichos*, popular sayings, to which the knight-errant reacts with disdain, saying they clog Sancho's thought process. By the time *El Quijote* appeared at the beginning of the seventeenth century, the language—Castilian having metamorphosed into Spanish—was stunningly malleable. It was a vehicle to explore the national character, as Cervantes brilliantly does in his pages. Of course, it was Cervantes himself, along with a handful of other *Siglo de Oro* authors, who expanded the possibilities. In doing so, they helped solidify its standing.

If *El Quijote* is masterful in its entirety, its first sentence is unforgettable: an extract, an Aleph, a microcosm. It is an astonishing exercise in concealment, hiding as much (or as little) as it reveals; it gives both purpose and traction to the narrative:

> *En un lugar de la Mancha, de cuyo nombre no quiero acordarme, no ha mucho tiempo que vivía un hidalgo de los de lanza en astillero, adarga antigua, rocín flaco y galgo corredor.*

With only thirty-three words Cervantes invokes an entire universe. Millions know it by heart. A poll done in 2004 by the Spanish newspaper *El Mundo* revealed it was the best-known literary first line in Spain. Here is Ormsby's translation:

In a village of La Mancha, the name of which I have no desire to call to mind, there lived not long since one of those gentlemen that keep a lance in the lance-rack, an old buckler, a lean hack, and a greyhound for coursing.

There is a fairy-tale quality to the way that world is being portrayed, a kind of "Once upon a time" that enables the reader to nonetheless settle on a specific time, place, and individual.

Specific but not specified, for the line raises more questions than it answers. For instance: Where is this region called La Mancha? What about the village itself? Why isn't the village named? How about the hidalgo? Who is he? Does he have a name? How old is he? What are the items listed meant to tell us about his character? How did he get them? Does he have any family? Friends? Is he a loner?

Borges found even just the first six words of *El Quijote* worthy of syntactical study. In his essay "An Investigation of the Word," collected in *El idioma de los argentinos* (1928), he wrote (in my translation):

> *En* [in]. This is not a whole world, but the promise of others to come. It indicates that what immediately follows is not the main point in this context, but rather the location of the main point, be it in time or in space.
>
> *Un* [a]. Properly speaking, this word declares the unity of the word it modifies. Here it does not. Here it announces a real existence, but one not particularly individuated or demarcated.
>
> *Lugar* [place]. This is the word of location, promised by the particle "in." Its task is merely syntactical, not add-

ing any representation to the one suggested by the two previous words. To represent oneself "in" and to represent oneself "in a place" is the same, as any "in" is in a place and implies this. You will reply that *place* is a noun, a thing, and that Cervantes did not write it to signify a portion of space but rather to mean "hamlet," "town," or "village." To the first, I will respond that it is risky to allude *to things in themselves*, after Mach, Hume, and Berkeley, and, that, for a sincere reader, there is only a difference of emphasis between the preposition *in* and the noun *place*; in response to the second, the distinction is true, but only discernible later.

De [of]. The word is usually dependent, indicating possession. Here it is synonymous (somewhat unexpectedly) with *in*. Here it means that the scene of the still mysterious central statement of this clause is situated in turn somewhere else, which will be immediately revealed to us.

La [the]. This quasi-word (they tell us) is a derivation of *illa*, which means "that" in Latin. That is, it was first a word of orientation, justified and almost animated by some gesture; now it is a ghost of *illa*, with no further task than to indicate a grammatical gender, an extremely asexual classification which ascribes virility to pins (*"los" alfileres*) and not to laces (*"las" lanzas*). (By the way, it is fitting to recall what Graebner wrote about grammatical gender: Nowadays the opinion prevails that, originally, the grammatical genders represented a scale of values, and that the feminine gender represents, in many languages—among them the Semitic—a value inferior to the masculine.)

Mancha. The name is variously representable. Cervantes wrote it so that its known reality would lend
weight to the unheard-of reality of his Don Quixote. The
ingenious nobleman has paid back the debt with invest-
ment: if the nations of the world have heard of La Mancha, it is his doing.

Does this mean that La Mancha was nominated
because it already was a landscape for the novelist's contemporaries? I dare to assert the contrary: its reality was
not visual, but sentimental: it was, irrevocably, irrecon-
cilably, a dull provincial reality.

Borges's exegesis is engaging. His objective was to reduce to
its linguistic essence what is arguably the most famous sentence of the Spanish language. The part that Borges leaves out,
however, and one that is quite important, isn't conveyed in any
of the words of the sentence. That is that the protagonist of
El Quijote is devoid of a life story. In other words, the hidalgo
has no history. Or if he does, that history isn't conveyed to us.
The reader doesn't know anything about his birth, his parents,
his education, the cathartic experiences that define him. . . .
Instead, we get him *in medias res*: at midpoint, without antecedents, having come to life, in literary terms, fully formed.

ANOTHER FAMOUS CHARACTER without antecedents, coming from nowhere, is Gregor Samsa. It is possible that Kafka
was trying to imitate Cervantes's aesthetic strategy in his first
sentence of *Die Verwandlung* (1915), in English *The Metamor-*

phosis. The similarity doesn't appear to be coincidental given Kafka's wholehearted admiration for Cervantes (discussed further in chapter 8, "The Ebullient Bunch"). One might say that Kafka, in his novel, is doing exactly what Cervantes does in his: simultaneously revealing and concealing. In German, *The Metamorphosis* reads:

> *Als Gregor Samsa eines Morgens aus unruhigen Träumen erwachte, fand er sich in seinem Bett zu einem ungeheuren Ungeziefer verwandelt.*

This is Willa and Edwin Muir's translation:

> As Gregor Samsa awoke one morning from uneasy dreams he found himself transformed in his bed into a gigantic insect.

The reader doesn't know who Gregor Samsa is, his age, his physical features, what prompted such mutation, why he suffers from uneasy dreams, or if the dreams are the cause of his transformation. Other questions remain similarly unanswered: Is the fact that he is in bed, waking up, significant? And what kind of self-discovery is involved in the act of finding himself transformed into the insect? Vladimir Nabokov, who also lectured on Kafka's novel and who was a collector of *Lepidoptera*, added yet another question: what kind of insect does Samsa become?

As in *The Metamorphosis*, the protagonist of *El Quijote* is an individual without a past. That past is absent from the start and remains annulled in the entire narrative. The hidalgo who is soon to become a knight-errant comes to us already as a seasoned, mature man. Keeping him without a past is an intriguing device. In Cervantes's time, individuals were to a large degree still defined by their family. Professions were passed from one generation to the next, which meant that everyone was a "son of" somebody. Not exploring the protagonist's past might be a way to acknowledge a transitional moment in which identity began to shift in favor of one that individuals had to craft for themselves. But it might also be a nod by Cervantes to the role the Spanish Inquisition played in the early seventeenth century, persecuting those whose blood lineage was tarnished by either Jewish or Muslim ancestry.

It isn't accidental that the town where the action of *El Quijote* takes place isn't mentioned. Nor is it unintentional that when the hidalgo's name is actually offered, in the paragraph that follows, its spelling is delivered in the most uncertain of terms. We are told that his surname (*su sobrenombre*) is Quijada, which in Spanish means "jaw," or Quesada, but that some people accept the common spelling of his name to be *Quejana*.

In English translations, the surnames have undergone yet another layer of changes. John Ormsby, for instance, renders the sentence about onomastics, the science of names, thus: "They will have it his surname was Quixada or Quesada (for here there is some difference of opinion among the authors who write on the subject), although from reasonable conjectures it seems plain that he was called Quexana."

On the topic of onomastics, being evasive—suggesting the narrative is authored by different individuals and being confusing about its concrete details—was a custom in chivalry novels. At the heart of this tradition was a myth, a heroic character whose qualities aren't of this world. Myths cannot be accounted for in earthly, straightforward fashion, since they are subject to speculation.

But onomastic evasiveness is also linked to *La Convivencia*, a period when people sought ways to hide their genealogy, to be elusive about their family tree, particularly when information might lead to questions of Jewish or Muslim ancestry. Indeed, it's this obliqueness that makes some suspect Cervantes of being a *converso*.

In any case, Don Quixote's identity would become so famous as to enter the global lexicon as a new word: *quixotic*. Indeed, if *El Quijote* has a total of 381,104 words, and if Cervantes's lexicon was made up of 22,939 different words, there is one word alone, one frequently—and insidiously—attached to Cervantes's novel but thoroughly absent from its pages. That word is *quijotesco*, an adjective that in English is taken to mean—erroneously—"quixotic."

To understand the vicissitudes of the adjective, the life it has enjoyed across centuries, is to begin to appreciate the magisterial impact the novel has had in the entire world.

In *The Devil's Dictionary* (1911), Ambrose Bierce, known for his acerbic humor, defines *quixotic* as "absurdly chivalric, like Don Quixote." "An insight into the beauty and excellence of this incomparable adjective," he adds, "is unhappily denied to him who has the misfortune to know that the gentleman's name [in English] is pronounced *Ke-ho-tay*." Bierce is of course being fanciful, for *quixotic* doesn't mean "absurdly chivalric," unless the expression is taken to mean "idealistic." *Quixotic*, in fact, is an attribute of unreality, used not in derogatory terms but benevolently. It refers to the capacity to act against the current, to pursue one's dreams against all odds, to be stubbornly impractical.

Etymologically, *quijotesco* has undergone an evolution easy to trace. It shows up in Sebastián de Covarrubias Orozco's *Tesoro de la lengua castellana o española* (1611), the second Spanish-language dictionary ever published. The first, by Antonio de Nebrija, was released in 1492, the same year Columbus crossed the Atlantic. Covarrubias was not only a lexicographer, but also a cryptographer, a mortalist, and a translator of Horace into Spanish. Not much is known about him, but judging from his haphazard definitions in the *Tesoro* (he defined *sucio*, dirty, in a single line as "he who isn't clean," whereas he devotes eleven pages to *elefante*, elephant), one can conclude that he wasn't much of a consistent, stylized lexicographer, like Samuel Johnson was.

The *Tesoro* came out six years after the First Part of *El Quijote*. It records the word *quijotes*, but the definition Covarrubias gives has nothing to do with the novel, or almost nothing. He describes *quijote* as the part of a suit of armor covering the tights, suggesting that Cervantes took the word and made it into a proper name rather than the reverse—that is, that *quijote* was part of the vocabulary before Cervantes made use of it for his character. There is no record of Covarrubias having read Cervantes's novel. If he did, he didn't appear to find anything worthy of mention in it.

Published more than a century later, the *Diccionario de autoridades* (1737) lists the following items (my translation): *quixotada*: A ridiculously serious action, or to be determined to do something without having a purpose; *quixote*: A ridiculously serious man, or determined in doing what does not correspond to him; and *quixotería*: A ridiculous mode or demeanor, or determination to achieve a goal.

In other words, from Covarrubias to *Autoridades*, the adjective went from a word unrelated to *El Quijote* to a series of nouns making direct reference to it.

In its 2001 edition of *Diccionario de la lengua española*, the *Real Academia Española* listed a handful of other terms, among them *quijotescamente*, an adverb; *quijotil*, a variation on the noun *quijotesco*; and *quijotismo*, the faculty of being quixotic.

A similar journey to the one I'm describing in Spanish is traceable in French (*quixotic*), Italian (*donchisciottesco*; the Italians, with their love of honorifics, add the "don"), Portuguese (*quixotesco*), Basque (*quixotic*), Catalan (*quixotesc*), Japanese (非現実的な), Yiddish (קוויקסאטיש), Polish (*donkiszotowski*), and Russian (донкихотский), to name a few languages. The adjective is recorded in dictionaries in these languages at different points toward the end of the nineteenth century and beyond, as *El Quijote* became an international classic and its protagonist a household name among artists, intellectuals, and politicians.

In English, the vicissitudes of *quixotic* are just as emblematic. *The Oxford English Dictionary* claims that the word first appeared in print in Shakespeare's tongue in 1648, that is, more than three decades after the First Part was translated by Thomas Shelton and published in London.

In its 1971 edition, the *OED* included three words: *Quixote*, *quixotic*, and *quixotry*. It defined *quixotic* as "1. Of persons: resembling Don Quixote; hence, striving with lofty enthusiasm for visionary ideas." Here the lexicon tones down its judgmental voice, connecting enthusiasm with vision but without criticizing such an attitude. And "2. Of actions, undertakings, etc. Characteristic of, appropriate to, Don Quixote." Finally, the *OED* offers another word I'm unfamiliar with: *quixotry*. The lexicon fails to explain it. It might simply be a noun version of *quixotic*, that is, actions that are quixotic.

In contrast, the eleventh (1983) edition of *Merriam-Webster's Collegiate Dictionary*, which stands as the American response to the *OED* (less lofty and more practical), defines *quixotic* not as ridiculous but as "foolishly impractical," "marked by rash lofty romantic ideas or extravagant chivalrous action," and "capricious, unpredictable." It offers an adverb too: *quixotically*. And it gives several examples, among which is this one: "In this age of giant chain stores, any attempt at operating an independent bookstore must be regarded as quixotic." The lexicon follows its statement with a handful of synonyms: *idealistic, quixotical, romantic, starry, starry-eyed, utopian,* and *visionary*. Some of these are as far-fetched in regard to Don Quixote's character as Bierce's definition and the indulgences of the *OED*. *Merriam-Webster's* also includes *quixotical*, another word I haven't a clue about.

This etymological history, in Spanish, English, and other languages, leads to a single, shocking fact: in all of the Western canon, no other novelistic character has ever been adjectivized. That is, neither in the *Diccionario de la lengua española* nor in the *OED* are there listings for *odyssean, macbethian, kareninean,* or *buendían*. On the other hand, famous authors' surnames are frequently adjectivized: *Brechtian, Kafkaesque, Joycean, Orwellian,* and so on.

Cervantes, in English, has never given place to the *Cervantean*. But it has in Spanish: *cervantesco* and *cervantino*, a reference to a labyrinthine, perhaps even solipsistic approach to life. This means that Cervantes, for people in the Hispanic world, is a titan. He no doubt is important elsewhere, but it is *El Quijote*, and not its author, that matters most in other habitats.

By the way, there is ambiguity in Spanish between *Quijote* and *Quixote*, that is, between the *x* and the *j*. The same ambiguity is present in a handful of other words, including in *Mexico*.

Until 1810 or thereabouts, when Mexico became an independent nation, the word was spelled with a *j*, as was *Tejas*. In the case of *Mexico*, the change resulted from a series of factors, including an effort to indigenize the country's identity. Symbolically, that is, for aesthetic and psychosocial reasons, the *x* was seen as representing Aztec culture.

In his *Tesoro*, Covarrubias spells the word *Quixotes*, in plural and with an *x*, not with a *j*. When Covarrubias compiled his dictionary, at a time when Cervantes was contemplating the Second Part, spelling in the Spanish language was nothing if not anarchic. Letters like *x* and *j*, *s* and *z*, weren't always stable. The *Diccionario de la lengua española* endorses Cervantes's preferred *j* spelling, settling the issue for good.

Ambrose Bierce makes fun of the rather bizarre pronunciation in English, *Ke-ho-tay*, thus signaling the way translations of the novel exoticized the protagonist's name by replacing the *j* with an *x*. The first translators of *El Quijote* sought to Anglicize the orthography of Spanish names in order to respect, to the degree possible, the original phonetics. To them, *Quixote* sounded better than *Quijote* because the *j* would have given place to *Quiyote*. (By the way, Burton Raffel, one of the twenty English-language translators of *El Quijote*, spells the name *Don Quijote*—with the *j*—throughout, to seek authenticity and to distinguish himself from the previous translators.)

By creating an adjective out of the name *Don Quixote*, the characteristics of Cervantes's knight-errant acquired universal status. It is astonishing how malleable *quixotic* has become, used to describe almost anyone who battles an established order. I have seen it attached to famous figures like Columbus, Galileo, Spinoza, Marx, Freud, David Ben-Gurion, Mao

Zedong, Ernesto "Che" Guevara, and, most recently, Nelson Mandela. The adjective is also applicable to other literary creations. Huckleberry Finn is quixotic. Dostoyevsky's Prince Myshkin is too, as are Jacques *le fataliste*, Captain Ahab, and Emma Bovary. And maybe Hamlet.

Of course, there is an anachronistic quality to this last comparison. Chronologically, Hamlet can't be quixotic since Shakespeare's play was written in 1599, six years before the First Part of *El Quijote* was published. But chronology is often the least of concerns for readers, for whom literature is timeless. All characters, regardless of their origin, exist in the dimension of the ever-present.

Ironically, the adjective *quixotic* doesn't stick to Cervantes himself. *Cervantesco* and *cervantino* invoke specific characteristics connected with his work: a penchant for theatricality, a passion for irony, and an embrace of the various registers of language. In other words, he savored the ridiculous in life. But he wasn't ridiculous himself.

The question—to be pondered in the following section, "The World"—is how the adjective *quixotic* became an ideology, originally in Spain but soon thereafter throughout the entire Hispanic world, and how that ideology mutated over time.

THE WORLD

SECTION TWO

6

QUIJOTISMO AND *MENARDISMO*

n its full splendor, *El Quijote* not only has given birth to an adjective but also has become a doctrine, an ideology dictating the way people ought to live their lives. What exceptionalism and the American Dream are to the United States (more about that later), this ideology—*Quijotismo*—is to Spain and its former colonies across the Atlantic. Its central tenet is the implicit concept of rebellion: paraphrasing Montaigne, to sacrifice one's life for a dream is to know its true worth.

Another doctrine in the Hispanic world derived from Cervantes's novel is *Menardismo*, which is an outgrowth of Borges's famous story "Pierre Menard, Author of the *Quixote*." In this tale, written in the style of a book review, a nineteenth-century French Symbolist dreams of rewriting—not copying, but rewriting word by word—*El Quijote*. And he succeeds in his task: Cervantes's original and Menard's rewriting, when shown side by side, are identical; yet they are also different because the meaning of the words used by Cervantes and Menard has changed from the early seventeenth to the late nineteenth century. The unnamed narrator in Borges's story then argues not only that the two versions should be seen as having the same aesthetic value but also that they are—and here is Borges's most astonishing, inventive point—equally original. And the narrator makes the case that, as Menard's effort shows, the only way to read literature is contextually. By using Menard as an endorser of derivative art as authentic, Borges therefore announces that the former colonies known today as the Spanish-speaking Americas, while arriving late to the banquet of Western civilization, are as original in their derivative culture as Europe is.

To understand how *Quijotismo* evolved, it is necessary to understand the history of the novel's reception in the Hispanic world. After the defeat of the Armada in 1588, the Spanish Empire, which was really a federation of separate realms, underwent a period of decline. *El Quijote* might be said to have foreshadowed it in its exploration of the way that individuals, as well as an entire nation, are trapped in self-perpetuating delusions. V. S. Pritchett, the British novelist who had a lifelong fascination with Spain and wrote the book *The Spanish Temper* (1954), understood this conundrum. "*Don Quixote* has been called the novel that killed a country by knocking the heart out of it and extinguishing its belief in itself for ever," he wrote in a review of Samuel Putnam's translation of *Don Quixote* in the *New Yorker*. "The argument might really be the other way on. *Don Quixote* was written by the poor soldier and broken tax-collector with the hand maimed in his country's battles because the Spanish dream of Christian chivalry and total power has passed the crisis of success. The price of an illusion was already being paid and Cervantes marked it down."

In its first two centuries, the novel was seen as mere entertainment in Spain; its cast, as endearing types that represented different aspects of Spanish culture. While it was considered a classic, it hadn't yet fostered the type of scholarly industry we are used to today. Nor was it used by politicians for rhetorical purposes. A radical break occurred shortly before 1905, the 300th anniversary of the publication of the First Part. In 1898 a catastrophic event took place, one that reshaped the fiber of Spain: in a war with the United States that came to be known in English as the Spanish-American War and in Spanish as the *Guerra del '98*, Spain lost control of its colonies Cuba and Puerto Rico, in the Caribbean Basin, and the Philippines, in the Pacific.

The Spanish Empire crumbled, its finances in disarray. The intellectuals of the *Generación del '98*, and their heirs, immersed themselves in a soul-searching effort to understand what had gone wrong, why a once-powerful country was now in decline. José Martínez Ruiz (better known as Azorín), Ángel Ganivet, Miguel de Unamuno, Pío Baroja, and Ramiro de Maeztu, among others, wondered what the future held and looked for what one of them described as a way *hacia la otra España*, toward another Spain. They turned to *El Quijote* for clues about Spain's future, finding the novel a kaleidoscope of psychohistorical interpretations.

In his essays *Idearium español* and *El porvenir de España*, translated into English as *Spain: An Interpretation* (1897), Ganivet debated the country's view of history. He believed that at the end of the nineteenth century, Spain was in agony, directionless, in a state of depression, which he related to Alonso Quijano. He wanted Spaniards to reclaim their destiny, to become quixotic again, although he believed nihilism was too ingrained in the collective psyche for an entrepreneurial spirit to return. Maeztu, in his book *Defensa de la hispanidad* (1934), approached the knight-errant as the seed of *la hispanidad*, the collective character of the entire Spanish-speaking world. Pío Baroja wrote pessimistic novels like *El árbol de la ciencia*, published in 1911 and rendered into English in the United States as *The Tree of Science*. Some of his characters are gloomy, skeptical to the degree of becoming antisocial, even misanthropic. Infatuated with the knight-errant's adventures, Azorín, in *La ruta de Don Quijote*, traced the route of Don Quixote during a trip commissioned in 1905 by the director of the newspaper *El Imparcial*. He not only explored the geographical sites Cervantes included in *El Quijote* but also reflected on the role the book played in the collective imagination, arguing that Spain needed to use idealism as an antidote to its current state of pessimism.

Arguably, no author has been as obsessed with *El Quijote* as Unamuno. In his deeply Catholic view, the novel was timeless, the best contribution by Spain to civilization, one holding a clue to understanding the Iberian spirituality: the nation, he thought, was made of dreamers whose desire to live, to change things, had stagnated over the centuries as a result of an oppressive, corrupt Catholic Church that killed all forms of individuality and freedom. He believed it to be everlasting, its author unworthy of having written it, for such magisterial achievement could not be the result of human action. Unamuno understood the knight-errant as a model of passion. He thought this was also Jesus Christ's distinct characteristic. Passion, in his view, is what makes us believe in ourselves, what pushes us to fight for freedom and against injustice. He wanted people to be like Don Quixote and Jesus: to have faith in passion. Unamuno wrote, "The truth is that my work—I was going to say my mission—is to shatter the faith of men here, there, and everywhere, faith in affirmation, faith in negation, and faith in abstention in faith, and this for the sake of faith in faith itself; it is to war against all those who submit, whether it be to Catholicism, or to rationalism, or to agnosticism; it is to make all men live the life of inquietude and passionate desire."

When the war broke out, Unamuno wrote an essay called *"¡Muera Don Quijote!"* in which he argued that the character was an expression of a Romantic idea that had died with the country's disastrous military encounter. But Unamuno's love for the novel persisted. However, Unamuno's most famous book, one difficult to describe, is *Vida de Don Quijote y Sancho*, published in 1905 (it underwent successive editions, with prologues added in 1913 and 1928). Part autobiography, part novelistic disquisition, part guided tour of the novel, he used it to revive the spirit of the knight-errant as a collective force always pushing Spain forward.

Alongside these intellectuals is José Ortega y Gasset, younger in age and thus an heir of the *Generación del '98*, whose book *Meditations on Quixote* began articulating his theory that we're all products of our own environment, encapsulated in the maxim *"yo soy yo y mi circunstancia, y si no la salvo a ella no me salvo yo,"* I am I and my circumstance, and, if I do not save it, I do not save myself. Reading his vast oeuvre, one is able to trace the dialogue he established—at times directly, at others obliquely—with Cervantes's knight-errant as an archetype of the Spanish soul, from *The Revolt of the Masses* (1930) to his disquisitions on Diego Velázquez and Francisco Goya. In his opinion, *El Quijote* holds the secret to everything Spanish: its fatalism and intense faith. The novel, in the philosopher's eyes, is a manual for life. In *The Dehumanization of Art and Ideas about the Novel* (1925), he cautioned against *idées fixes*, an approach that is connected to his view of Don Quixote as a character who gives up the superfluous, embraces sincerity, and acts with conviction: "There is truth only in an existence which feels its acts as irrevocably necessary," Ortega y Gasset wrote. "There exists today no politician who feels the inevitableness of his policy, and the more extreme his attitudes, the more frivolous, the less inspired by destiny they are. The only life with its roots fixed in earth, the only autochthonous life, is that which is made of inevitable acts. All the rest, all that it is in our power to take or to leave or to exchange for something else, is mere falsification of life." In short, *Quijotismo* was a double-edged weapon: it portrayed the idealism of the knight-errant as proof that Spain was delusional about its past, yet it implied that only idealism might help the country out of its depression.

The ideology morphed into a kind of sport: depicting the knight-errant and his friends in times of trouble. These depictions are particularly vivid in art. *El Quijote* was a favorite subject of Goya, the famous late-eighteenth- and early-nineteenth-century Spanish painter, whom a few of the Generation of '98 intellectuals saw as a precursor. He drew the knight-errant on his horse, Rocinante, while Sancho is in the act of falling off his donkey, Rucio. The scene is reminiscent of Goya's paintings of the disasters of the Napoleonic wars. Goya presents the knight-errant as an opponent of dogmatism and a friend of the freedom of the imagination.

Yet the most ubiquitous, symbolically charged image of all, Spanish and otherwise, is a silhouette Pablo Picasso drew for the cover of the French weekly magazine *Les Lettres Françaises* in August 1955, in commemoration of the 350th anniversary of the publication of the First Part. At the top of the cover, a text reads, *"Don Quichotte, vu par Pablo Picasso,"* *El Quijote* through Picasso's eyes. Indisputably, no image of any novel is more famous.

In Picasso's drawing, Don Quixote is seen in emaciated profile, wearing his suit of armor, his helmet and shield, holding his spear with pride. To his left and in the background is his squire atop his donkey. If the knight-errant is skeletal, the squire is a ball of matter: rounded, insect-like. Scattered through the hilly landscape are four small windmills more or less evenly positioned, some more clearly depicted than others. And on the top left corner is the Spanish sun, iridescent, accompanying our friends wherever they go. What Picasso sees is stunningly simple. There is something melancholic, pathetic, even childish in his silhouette, as it should be.

Drawing of Don Quixote and Sancho (1955) by Pablo Picasso, arguably the most iconic of all images inspired by Cervantes's novel.

The silhouette has been appropriated by the government, as well as by corporations, as a logo for Spanish tourism. Since the 1970s it has often been reproduced on T-shirts, watches, posters, coffee mugs, dishes, and pencils, and even as tattoos. Today it is as ubiquitous as the iconography of Che Guevara, Eva Perón, Hugo Chávez, and other icons of the Hispanic world.

In 1915, to commemorate the 300th anniversary of the publication of the Second Part of *El Quijote*, and the death of Cervantes a year later, a contest was announced to create a large granite statue of the author, to be placed in the heart of Madrid, in the Plaza de España, at the western end of the Gran

Monument to Don Quixote and Sancho in Plaza de España, Madrid, erected in 1927.

Vía. The winning team included architects Rafael Martínez Zapatero and Pedro Muguruza, as well as sculptor Lorenzo Coullaut Valera. Funds were raised not only in Spain but also across the Americas. Work didn't begin until 1925, and the statue was first unveiled in unfinished form in 1929. The figure of Cervantes was completed in 1930. Funding for various other elements was lacking, so they were added over time, with work done in 1947 and 1956 by Federico Coullaut-Valera Mendigutia, son of the original sculptor, who added statues of Don Quixote and Sancho, Aldonza Lorenzo, and Dulcinea del Toboso.

WHILE ARGUABLY THE MOST FAMOUS, the sculpture at the Plaza de España is just one of hundreds of statues of Don Quixote and Sancho Panza around the globe, especially in Spanish-speaking countries, where almost every major metropolis has them, either in public spaces or inside museums. This is because *Quixotismo* also extended across the Atlantic into the former Spanish colonies, known from the mid-nineteenth century onward under the name *América Latina*.

However, the doctrine took a divergent shape there. For a long time Spain had been the oppressor, the enemy, yet the melancholia generated by its downfall was felt in the emerging republics as well, leading artists and writers at times to lament its decline. Even as they celebrated the dawn of a new era in which Spain would no longer be exerting its control across the Atlantic Ocean, these intellectuals were attracted to quixotism, seen not as a synonym of melancholia but as a liberating force, a doctrine promoting idealism.

The first time *El Quijote* was printed in the New World was in 1833, in Mexico City, in the form of Mariano Arevalo's five-volume edition. The novel's impact on the intelligentsia was palpable before, yet it achieved a benchmark some fifty years later when members of an intellectual movement known as *Modernismo* used the Spanish-American War, among other incidents, to define the fragmented cultures of the Americas as a galaxy united by the gravitational center of Spanish origins, despite other important influences that came from France, the United States, England, Germany, and even the Far East. For the first time, writers from countries like Nicaragua (Rubén Darío), Cuba (José Martí, Julián del Casal), Mexico (Amado Nervo, Enrique González Martínez, Manuel Gutiérrez Nájera), Argentina (Alfonsina Storni, Leopoldo Lugones), Uruguay (Delmira Agustini, Manuel González Prada), Colombia (José Asunción Silva), and Peru (José Santos Chocano) perceived themselves as unified, not only in their language but also in their worldview. The majority of them were poets, although some published fiction and journalism as well.

For the Latin American *Modernistas*, *Quijotismo* was about looking for the authentic, freedom-loving, forward-looking side of the former colonies as they embarked on a journey of self-definition. In 1905, to celebrate the 300th anniversary of the publication of the First Part of *El Quijote*, Rubén Darío, the undisputed leader of the *Modernistas*, wrote a commemorative poem, "*Letanía de nuestro señor Don Quijote*," litany for "our lord" Don Quixote. Published in Madrid, it asks the knight-errant to pray that the Spanish character endures. This is the most significant stanza:

> *Ruega generoso, piadoso, orgulloso;*
> *ruega casto, puro, celeste, animoso;*
> *por nos intercede, suplica por nos,*
> *pues casi ya estamos sin savia, sin brote,*
> *sin alma, sin vida, sin luz, sin Quijote,*
> *sin piel y sin alas, sin Sancho y sin Dios.*

Here is my own free translation:

> Beg for us generously, piously, proudly;
> beg chaste, pure, celestial, animated;
> intercede for us, appeal for us,
> for we're almost without sap, without bud,
> without soul, life, light, without Quixote;
> without skin and wings, without Sancho and God.

If Darío is the leader of the *Modernistas*, the movement's philosopher was the Uruguayan thinker José Enrique Rodó. In his book *Ariel*, he adopted—and adapted—*Quijotismo* for use in the Latin American context, never mentioning it directly yet using its essence to construct a view of the dialectics that shaped the temperament of the Americas.

The slim volume is structured as a letter to the youth of the Spanish Americas. He uses a central character from *The Tempest*, Shakespeare's last play (and, as such, his farewell to his years on the London stage), as the proponent of the Latin American embrace of its idealistic—and, therefore, quixotic—side. Ariel is an ethereal spirit, Prospero's ears and eyes. The counter-voice, a demon symbolizing brutishness, carnality, even materialism, is Caliban.

Ariel was published in 1900, two years after the end of the Spanish-American War and a year after another influential anti-imperialist work, Conrad's *Heart of Darkness*, appeared. The United States was now the hemispheric superpower, a force to reckon with in the Americas. In Rodó's view, Ariel represented Latin America, the idealist side of the continent, whereas Caliban was the United States, its materialistic other side.

People talk of *Arielismo* as a genuine Latin American philosophy, an effort to look at the New World through the prism of idealism. As such, *Arielismo* is an outgrowth of *Quijotismo*: a dreamer's dream.

Given the region's enthusiastic adoption and adaptations of *Quijotismo*, depictions of Don Quixote and Sancho, in popular as well as in highbrow culture, are as ubiquitous in Latin America as they are in Spain. My own favorite, also made in the early twentieth century, is José Guadalupe Posada's *Calavera Quijotesca* (1907), which depicts Don Quixote and Rocinante as skeletons. Posada is credited for having created the skulls that have become ubiquitous during *Día de los Muertos*, the Mexican Day of the Dead, the celebrations of which start on the first day of November. He was active during the more-than-thirty-year-long Porfirio Díaz dictatorship, which collapsed with the revolution of 1910. Posada's prophetic skeleton is an attempt at portraying the times he was living in as unreal and in desperate need of freedom to alleviate countless social ills.

Other representations abound, from cartoons and dances to television sketches and films. The most famous cinematic ones—and arguably the reason why millions of working-class people are familiar with *El Quijote* without having read it—are by Mario Moreno, the Mexican *carpero* comedian better known

Calavera Quijotesca *(c. 1910–13), engraving by José Guadalupe Posada, an artist "of the people" in Mexico whose work inspired Diego Rivera.*

as Cantinflas. He played the lead in the slapstick comedy *Don Quijote sin Mancha* (1969), directed by his longtime collaborator Miguel M. Delgado, and played Sancho to Spanish lead actor Fernando Fernán Gómez's knight-errant in *Don Quijote cabalga de nuevo* (1973).

It is interesting that, in contrast with Spain, adaptations of *El Quijote* in Latin America often come in the form of comedies. This might be because, at its core, the population uses humor, particularly in the twentieth century, as a way to confront disaster. In art, music, literature, and painting, laughter is seen as a medicine to combat the inclemencies of fate.

In the political realm, a number of legendary Latin American freedom fighters have modeled themselves after Don Quixote, chief among them Che Guevara, the Marxist rebel, who had read Cervantes's novel assiduously since he was a young man. When, at the age of twenty-three, as a medical student, he, along with his friend Alberto Granado, decided to traverse South America on motorcycle, they saw themselves as a flesh-and-bones replica of Don Quixote and Sancho. After bidding farewell to his friend Fidel Castro and to Cuba, a country to which he had helped to bring communism, and opting to continue his armed struggle throughout Latin America, he decided to travel to Bolivia, where he was eventually killed. On April 1, 1965, he wrote a letter to his Argentine parents, in which he stated, "Once again I feel beneath my heels the ribs of Rocinante. Once more, I'm on the road with my shield on my arm."

Similarly, Subcomandante Insurgente Marcos, the nom de guerre of Rafael Sebastián Guillén Vicente, who in 1994 led the rebel movement known as the Zapatista Army of National Liberation against the Mexican government and the U.S.-Mexico-Canada Free Trade Agreement, and who sought to reclaim the rights of indigenous people in the state of Chiapas, was an ardent Quixote fan. In an interview with Gabriel García Márquez and Roberto Pombo published in the Colombian magazine *Cambio* on March 25, 2001, El Sup, as he was affectionately known, still involved in his utopian armed struggle, described the knight-errant as his hero. "I received a hard-cover book as a present when I turned twelve years old. It was *Don Quixote of La Mancha*," he said. "I had already read it but in young-adult versions. It was an expensive volume, a special gift that must be waiting for me somewhere. Shakespeare arrived soon after."

In regard to the literature of the region, Cervantes's knight-errant has had an enormous impact. In the nineteenth century, a series of disquisitions and even a handful of rewritings of the novel appeared, among them—and most significantly— *Capítulos que se le olvidaron a Cervantes*, by the Ecuadorian writer Juan Montalvo. Published posthumously in 1895, it imagines a continuation of Don Quixote and Sancho's third outing. An independent-minded anticlerical thinker, Montalvo had a remarkable ability to mimic Cervantes's style and content. His narrative is the closest I know to a sequel that feels authentic. (Its title, in Spanish, suggests these to be the chapters—a total of sixty—Cervantes forgot to include when writing the Second Part.)

Gabriel García Márquez's *One Hundred Years of Solitude* (1967) is driven by the tension between the real and the imaginary. The influence of *Quijotismo* is everywhere apparent, from the presence of a palimpsest as a narrative device to the philosophical dichotomy that distinguishes the twins Aureliano and José Arcadio Buendía. In equal measure, other works by the Colombian author and Nobel Prize winner, such as *No One Writes to the Colonel* (1961), *The Autumn of the Patriarch* (1975), and *The General in His Labyrinth* (1989), feature protagonists who are undoubtedly quixotic in the way they inhabit their own reality.

Carlos Fuentes features aspects of *El Quijote* in his magnum opus *Terra nostra* and, to a lesser extent, in his thriller *The Hydra Head* (1978), about the Arab-Israeli conflict. In fact, in retrospect Fuentes (aside from Borges) might be the Latin American man of letters most devoted to *El Quijote*. In 1976, he published *Cervantes o la crítica de la lectura*, a book-long essay on *El Quijote* that looks at the novel as a critique of reading. In English, the piece appears in Fuentes's collection of essays *Myself with Others* (1990). In it, and in subsequent speeches and introductions, Fuentes portrayed Cervantes's novel as a tool that fosters democracy and fights intolerance because it is constantly making a critique of itself and "it wants to make real what history forgot." Fuentes particularly loved the self-referentiality in it. "It is a narrative," he argued, in which "we read a book about a man who reads books and then becomes a book about a man who knows that he is being read." This, in his view, is liberating in that it announced not only that characters are as real as people but that reading is an activity that has no boundaries:

> When Don Quixote enters the printing shop in Barcelona and discovers that what is being printed is his own book, *El ingenioso hidalgo Don Quijote de La Mancha*, we are suddenly plunged into a truly new world of readers, of readings available to all and not only to a small circle of power, religious, political or social.

There is also Roberto Bolaño, whose episodic road novel *The Savage Detectives*, about two Mexican hooligans, Arturo Belano and Ulises Lima, looking for a long-forgotten mythical female poet, might be read as a rewriting, in structure as well as in style, of Cervantes's masterpiece.

Unlike manifestations of *Quijotismo* in Spain, none of these artifacts have been used by others as a tool to explain, and even transform, reality—that is, as the source of an ideology. The one that does, and unquestionably the most important rethinking on this side of the Atlantic—and, as it happens, the shaping of a fresh ideological approach—is Borges's influential story "Pierre Menard, Author of the *Quixote*."

On Christmas Eve 1938, at age thirty-nine, Borges had an accident. As he was walking up a staircase in Buenos Aires, on his way to return a copy of *The Arabian Nights*, he smashed his forehead against an open window frame. The impact was severe. But he didn't pay attention to his bleeding head. He proceeded to his destination. It was only when the owner of the book heard Borges's knock and opened the door to his apartment that Borges saw the wound and realized how serious it had been. Soon thereafter, Borges lost consciousness. The episode served as inspiration for his autobiographical story "El sur."

Until this point, Borges was known as an avant-garde, cerebral poet as well as a book and film reviewer. His work was published in intellectual journals, although he wrote columns and features in women's magazines. It was on his poetry that he placed his bet to fame. The accident changed things.

Borges convalesced at the hospital. He feared his mental faculties, his capacity to remember, had been diminished. To test himself, he wrote a short story: "Pierre Menard, Author of the *Quixote*." It was not his first (in 1933, he had authored "*Hombre de la esquina rosada*"), but it was his most ambitious to date. Published in Victoria Ocampo's journal *Sur* in 1939 and included in the volume *Ficciones*, released in 1944, it is among the most influential stories of the twentieth century. It is also among Borges's most famous stories, which is no small feat given the reputation of many others, such as "The Library of Babel," "Tlön, Uqbar, Orbis Tertius," "The Circular Ruins," and "Death and the Compass."

As it turned out, "Pierre Menard, Author of the *Quixote*" didn't only prove the soundness of Borges's mind; it revolutionized our understanding of the crossroads where history and reading meet. And it offered fresh insight into the centrality of Cervantes's novel in the Hispanic world, and into the reconfiguration of Spanish culture as it continuously plays itself out in the Americas.

In truth, to call this a story is somewhat deceitful. Although a substantial portion of the content is fictional, Borges presents it as an essay, or perhaps a book review. In the story, the narrator (who may be the author himself, or not) sets out to analyze the work—the words—of a fictional late-nineteenth- and early-twentieth-century French Symbolist novelist, Pierre Menard. The narrator focuses on Menard's single most original contribution, as well as the most "absurd": the rewriting, though not the copying, of chapters IX and XXXVIII of the First Part of *El Quijote*.

As the narrator tells us, Menard "did not want to compose another *Quixote*—which is easy—but the *Quixote* itself." That is, he wanted to write it exactly as Cervantes had written it the first time around, not a single word of it different. The key term is *rescribir*, to rewrite: Menard does not copy Cervantes's novel word by word; he creates it all over again, meaning that, without a copy in front of him, he faithfully composes precisely the same text of 1605.

Not really. Borges's story is built on a Platonic concept of literature which suggests that masterpieces past, present, and future are intrinsic, universal features of Nature that exist before and after they become tangible to readers. The act of writing down is simply the human endeavor that unveils universal features, making them visible. ("Pierre Menard, Author of the *Quixote*" begins with a discussion of the difference between Menard's *visible* and *invisible* work.) Furthermore, those masterpieces, like *Don Quixote*, exist in spite of, and separate from, their creator. This means that if Cervantes was able to retrieve it, someone else might be able to do the same. Or, to use electronic jargon, Menard could download the classic, just as it had been downloaded more than three hundred years prior.

But who uploaded it, then? Menard's idea invokes an Emersonian concept of authorship: all individual writers are but transient, expiring aspects of a single Universal Mind, whose attributes summarize and encompass all the individualities available. In other words, that abstract Platonic Writer of Writers is the true and sole original author, and earthly incarnations (Cervantes, Menard, you, and I) are but scribes through whom the Universal Mind communicates its content.

In what is perhaps the most inspiring section of the piece— and of Borges's entire career—the narrator announces (in my translation, which incorporates a quote from the Ormsby rendition) this:

> It is a revelation to compare Menard's *Don Quixote* with Cervantes. The latter, for instance, wrote (*Don Quixote*, First Part, chapter IX):
>
> > . . . *truth, whose mother is history, rival of time, storehouse of deeds, witness for the past, example and counsel for the present, and warning for the future.*
>
> Composed in the seventeenth century, composed by the "lay genius" Cervantes, this enumeration is a mere rhetorical praise of history. Menard, instead, writes:

. . . truth, whose mother is history, rival of time, store-
house of deeds, witness for the past, example and coun-
sel for the present, and warning for the future.

History, *mother* of truth; the idea is astonishing. Menard, a contemporary of William James, doesn't define history as an inquiry into reality but as its origin. Historical truth, for him, isn't what happened; it is what we judge to have happened. The final causes—*example and counsel for the present, and warning for the future*—are brazenly pragmatic.

The contrast in styles is also vivid. Menard's archaic style—he is, in the end, a foreigner—suffers from a certain affectation. This isn't the case of his precursor, who uninhibitedly handles the current Spanish of his time.

The words are identical, yet the meaning is different. Borges's story offers a double critique: of originality as an artistic objective (nothing human is really original, only the Universal Mind), and of the act of reading (the exact same quote is understood quite differently depending on the time in which it is framed).

This suggests that *Don Quixote* is a fixed text but that no two readers of it look at it the same way, for individuals bring to the material subjective views. The novel, therefore, is not one but many—as many as the readers who interpret it and, as in the case of Menard, the writers who attempt to rewrite it.

But if there are so many classics, products of a Universal Mind, that have inspired countless interpretations, why does Menard choose to rewrite *Don Quixote*? "Two texts of unequal value inspired this undertaking," the narrator states. "One is that philosophical fragment by Novalis—the one numbered 2005 in the Dresden edition—which outlines the theme of a *total* identification with a given author." That is, Menard identifies completely with Cervantes, to the point of becoming his doppelgänger. "The other is one of those parasitic books which situate Christ on a boulevard, Hamlet on Le Cannobière or Don Quixote on Wall Street. Like all men of good taste, Menard abhorred these useless carnivals, fit only—as he would say— to produce the plebeian pleasure of anachronism or (what is worse) to enthrall us with the elementary idea that all epochs are the same or are different." Menard is insistent on avoiding such anachronisms.

Menard could have chosen another Iberian literary landmark: *El Cid*, *The Lazarillo of Tormes*, or *La Celestina*. However, these books are contingent on the Spanish tradition, but they are not superior to it; that is, they are part of history, not above it. *El Quijote* is the *ur*-text, the fountainhead, the book that gives legitimacy to this tradition. One could imagine Spanish letters without *La Celestina*; but Spain itself, as concept and reality, would not exist without *El Quijote*.

There is another relevant question worth asking: Why does Borges make Pierre Menard a Frenchman? Why not a Spaniard rewriting the contemporary Spanish *ur*-text? That—to quote Menard again—would have been too easy, since the very definition of tradition is "the transmission of customs or beliefs from one generation to another within a particular context." In their writing, all German writers, consciously and otherwise, respond to Goethe.

By placing Menard out of the Spanish-language cultural

orbit, the story not only reflects on individual ways of reading; it is about modernity as a fractured condition. To rewrite *Don Quixote*, Menard needed "to know Spanish well, recover the Catholic faith, fight against the Moors or the Turks, forget the history of Europe between the years 1602 and 1918, *be* Miguel de Cervantes." The narrator adds that "he attained a fairly accurate command of 17th-century Spanish." He almost needed to cease being French and become a Spaniard.

The fact that Borges insinuates that a Frenchman—and, let us remember, France was idealized by Iberians and Hispanic Americans during the *Modernista* period at the end of the nineteenth century—might become the author, for example, the conduit, the proprietor of the most important Spanish book ever written, is unquestionably humorous. It also suggests a radical metamorphosis akin to the one undergone by immigrants: a person from one culture can become a full-fledged member of another. The suggestion is stunning. Latin America, after all, is a habitat shaped by an assortment of foreign cultures.

So do classics have a nationality? Do they belong to a particular nation? I argued earlier that classics are the mythology around which nations come together. That, certainly, is the case of Cervantes's novel, around which an entire civilization was built. But it could also be said that, regardless of their origin, classics are part of a universal reservoir without particular ownership. They're owned by everyone and no one. Hence, *El Quijote*—in Cervantes's delivery—is only accidentally Iberian, just as Faust is fortuitously German.

No Spaniard could have come up with such a declaration. Moreover, no Spaniard or Frenchman could have written

"Pierre Menard, Author of the *Quixote*." It could only have been a Latin American, for the region (like Africa, the Middle East, and other former colonies) is known as a manufacturer of copies, duplicates, and rewrites. Only an Argentine could dream of making unoriginality original.

Therein lies my theory of *Menardismo*: the capacity to be inventive in a landscape where most of what is considered authentic comes from abroad. The history of the Spanish-speaking world is the history of its lack of originality. As Cervantes's novel was published, the empire went into a period of political, economic, and cultural decline from which it is finally emerging. Science had come from the outside and wasn't a native by-product. In contrast, the arts have been an essential, ongoing feature of Latin American cultures. And those arts are derivative in nature. Menard gives Latin American artists permission to copy others with such savvy that the results are original.

The number of *Menardistas* in Latin America, particularly in the literary realm, is substantial. From the "Boom" writers of the 1960s (Julio Cortázar, García Márquez, Mario Vargas Llosa, and others) to the McOndo generation of the 1990s and beyond (Jorge Volpi, Andrés Neuman, Juan Villoro, and so on), the desire to reuse foreign genres and themes in order to reinterpret, to revamp them, runs deep.

For instance, the iconography used by the Catholic Church in the New World mixes aboriginal elements of pre-Columbian religions. Likewise, the socialist revolutions in Chile, Uruguay, Venezuela, and other countries in the region show the way a political theory is infused with autochthonous elements to create an original fusion. The examples are truly endless.

Think of the way chocolate was first cultivated in the Americas, and then repackaged in Europe, only to be once again reinvented as a culinary delicacy in Mexico. Or the *canción de protesta*, the ballads that emerged as part of the Cuban Revolution, which are seen as adaptations of the chants of the French troubadour and other foreign forms into the local reality. The drive to be original in unoriginality, the instinct not to be constrained by the psychological role of the subaltern, is in the air people breathe, in the way they bow to imperial powers.

The historical impact of *Quijotismo* and *Menardismo* has taken forking paths. Whereas the former, a reaction to Spain's collective depression after the Spanish-American War, pushed the country and its satellites into a soul-searching process that resulted in an unrealistic view of its standing as a post-imperial power in the modern world, the latter was a liberating force allowing people to turn the colonial mentality on its head.

7

SHAKESPEARE'S QUIXOTE

id Cervantes know of Shakespeare's work? How about the other way around: did Shakespeare read *El Quijote*?

For years it was believed that Shakespeare and Cervantes died the exact same day: April 23, 1616. But this is inaccurate because Spain was already living under the Gregorian calendar at the beginning of the seventeenth century, whereas England still followed the Old Style Julian calendar. This means that Cervantes died a day before Shakespeare.

Cervantes was Shakespeare's elder by seven years. His imagination is centrifugal, moving away from its center, wandering around a topic, whereas the Bard's is centripetal, contracting rather than expanding, pulling itself toward a gravitational core. The novelist was a soldier before he became a writer. He left Spain for Italy and, on his way back, was taken prisoner in

Algiers. In contrast, the playwright went from his hometown Stratford-on-Avon to London, only one hundred miles away. He never ventured farther than that, in spite of the fact that several of his plays are set in other domains, including Italy (*Two Gentlemen of Verona* [between 1589 and 1592], *Romeo and Juliet* [1597], *The Merchant of Venice* [1605], and, in part, *Taming of the Shrew* [1593] and *Coriolanus* [between 1605 and 1608], among others), Denmark (*Hamlet* [between 1599 and 1602]), and a Caribbean island (*The Tempest* [1611]).

Shakespeare included a number of Spanish characters in his plays. Cervantes's interest in England appears to be minimal, although he sets the plot of one of the *Exemplary Novellas*, called *La española*, or *La española inglesa*, in Elizabeth I's England. Despite their differences, there exists a peculiar link between the two authors, what might be seen not as a debt of one to the other but as a borrowing of sorts.

In one of the episodes in the First Part of *El Quijote*, the knight-errant and his squire come across a disheveled character called Cardenio in the Sierra Morena. Sometime later, they listen to a priest relate the story of two characters, Cardenio and Lucinda, to a group assembled in the inn of Juan Palomeque. In the story, Cardenio, in a state of depression, living half-naked behind trees, describes his love for Lucinda and how he asked her father for her hand in marriage. But before her father even answered, Cardenio postponed the arrangement, having been asked by Duke Ricardo for his services. Soon a third character is introduced in the story, the conniving Don Fernando, who is the son of Duke Ricardo. Cardenio tells how Don Fernando, who read Cardenio's love letters and other writings to Lucinda, took advantage of him by usurping Lucinda in marriage. The

story continues beyond the inn as Sancho and other characters in *El Quijote* find Cardenio again in the Sierra Morena. He
describes how Lucinda secretly told him she wasn't ready to
marry Don Fernando, yet he heard her say, "I do," in the cer-
emony, which pushed him to despair.

Cervantes adapted the story from an episode in Ariosto's
Orlando furioso. As mentioned previously, paying tribute to
one's predecessors by reworking their plots was not uncommon
during the Renaissance. Over the centuries, criticism has been
made that the episode has little to do with the rest of the narrative in *El Quijote*: Cardenio, Lucinda, and Don Fernando don't
show up anywhere else in the novel. For some, this intrusion
is a sign of Cervantes's laziness (he probably had the novella
written down already) and carelessness (he didn't make any
effort to integrate it into the whole). But others praise it as a
tale within a tale in the tradition of *The Arabian Nights*.

Interestingly, Shakespeare collaborated with English dramatist John Fletcher (1579–1625) on at least two plays, *Henry
VIII* (published in 1623) and *The Two Noble Kinsmen*. Fletcher
authored about fifteen plays of his own and collaborated on
others with several contemporaries. One of those collaborations was called *The History of Cardenio*. It was staged in the
Royal Palace in 1613. The script was lost, however, and no one
seemed to have known what the play was about.

Then in 1994, Charles Hamilton, a handwriting expert who
specialized in lost manuscripts, suggested that the play had
been retitled *The Second Maiden's Tragedy*, which survives in
manuscript form and whose authorship has been attributed to
various Jacobean playwrights such as Thomas Goffe, George
Chapman, Thomas Middleton, and—yes!—William Shake-

speare. While using characters with names different from those in the Cardenio story of *El Quijote* (Lucinda becomes Lady, Fernando becomes Tyrant, and so on), the plot of the five-act play, according to Hamilton, is basically the same. He attributed it to Shakespeare, basing his thesis on a comparative analysis of Shakespeare's style.

Thomas Shelton, the first translator of *El Quijote* into English, completed the First Part in 1607. Although it wasn't published until 1612, it may have circulated first in manuscript form. In any case, when it was finally released, it quickly became a success. Is *The Second Maiden's Tragedy* proof that Shakespeare himself read *El Quijote*? (Hamilton thinks the Shelton translation reached Shakespeare in manuscript form in 1611.) And that he and his collaborator Fletcher were impressed enough to transpose it onto the stage? Or might it be that only Fletcher was acquainted with it, and that the role Shakespeare had in the collaboration was to simply add a few lines here and there or perhaps a scene or two?

The history of the play *Cardenio* gets even more complicated. In 1727, a British author and editor by the name of Lewis Theobald announced that he had in his possession not one but three manuscripts of Shakespeare and Fletcher's lost play about Cardenio. (It was said that Theobald wasn't able to publish Shakespeare's original manuscript because in the early part of the eighteenth century, copyright of the Bard's plays was in the hands of Jacob Tonson, an English publisher and bookseller who obtained it by buying the rights from the publisher of the Fourth Folio.) Theobald staged the play as *Double Falsehood, or the Distressed Lovers*. The plot is loosely based on the characters of Cervantes's *Ill-Conceived Curiosity*, though some names are altered. Skepticism about the authenticity of the material prevails to this day, and the play isn't particularly inspiring. While Theobald is also known as one of the editors of Shakespeare's works, this created a tension between him and Alexander Pope, the famous poet of *The Dunciad* (1728), who also edited the Bard's plays. They became enemies. Pope ridiculed Theobald as the first avatar of Dulness in *The Dunciad*.

The Arden Shakespeare, among the most authoritative editions of the Bard's work, included *Double Falsehood* in a 2010 edition by Brean Hammond. The insertion of the play into the canon wasn't greeted with universal enthusiasm. Some Shakespeare scholars believed the effort was premature, with more historical evidence needed to make the case for inclusion. A year later, the Royal Shakespeare Company presented a play called *Cardenio: Shakespeare's "Lost Play" Re-imagined* (2011), directed by Gregory Doran. The endeavor sought to synthesize different sources to approximate what the Bard and his collaborator might have had in mind. Of course, the concoction was, in principle, speculative.

In the end, literary historians believe the content of *Cardenio* is closer to Fletcher than to the Bard, with only a few flashes of his talent sprinkled in. Literary scholar Harold Bloom doesn't believe Hamilton's theory about Shakespeare being influenced by *El Quijote*. Along with other critics, he is skeptical that Shakespeare even read *El Quijote*, though, if he did, "we can surmise his delight," he argues, adding, "I doubt [Cervantes] would have valued Falstaff and Hamlet." Bloom once described Shakespeare as "the inventor of the human." If this is the case, Cervantes must be "the discoverer of doubt."

Would anything be different in literary history if these two giants knew of one another? It is unlikely. When Cervantes died, he himself wasn't aware of the reach of his oeuvre. He couldn't have imagined that, over the next centuries, he would be turned into a fountainhead. Nor could Shakespeare. Although he appears to have been more aware of the impact his work had in London, at the time of his death few of his plays had been staged abroad (*Romeo and Juliet*, in a shortened version, was performed in Nördlingen, in Bavaria, Germany, in 1604, but the first translations of the plays weren't produced in French and German until the second half of the eighteenth century). In other words, Shakespeare then wasn't the Shakespeare who is now universal.

Of course, neither was Cervantes *the* Cervantes.

8

THE EBULLIENT BUNCH

s is apparent by now, *El Quijote* is a mirror: its implications, its lessons always in the eyes of the beholder. To some, the novel is a manifesto for human freedom; to others, it is a treatise on psychiatry. Eternally fluid in its message, it can be seen to advocate individualism or collectivism, to view human nature as resilient or malleable. Therein, perhaps, lies the reason for its continued success.

The *El Quijote* fan club has, over the centuries, become extraordinarily far-reaching. Its proponents are an ebullient bunch, jovially finding new and intriguing viewpoints on the novel. Members include composers, lithographers, playwrights, opera librettists, painters, filmmakers, and even creators of video games. Many of the fans are inspired, some are even brilliant, and a few, such as Flaubert, Dostoyevsky, and Kafka, are recognized as geniuses.

To begin tracing the path of such a book club across cultures, it is important to invoke, once again, chapter LXXIII of the Second Part, which is also the novel's last. In it, the narrator, considering Don Quixote in his deathbed, announces:

> For me alone was Don Quixote born, and I for him; it was his to act, mine to write; we two together make but one.

Cervantes was reacting, in part, to the appropriation of his characters by the pseudonymous Alonso Fernández de Avellaneda, who beat him to releasing a sequel. But by claiming the knight-errant as his "alone" here, his possession, his avatar, Cervantes seems to be deterring future impostors from taking advantage of his creation.

He had little luck. Almost since his death, world literature has been filled with pseudo-sequels, adaptations, and re-creations, as well as tributes and celebrations. In 2004, Howard Mancing, who teaches at Purdue University in Lafayette, Indiana, published a two-volume *Cervantes Encyclopedia*, seeking to catalogue these Quixote-inspired creations, at least nominally. Not that it is possible, given the seemingly infinite number of references.

Unquestionably among the most passionate of the ebullient bunch were the Romantics, first in Germany, a country that came rather late to the banquet of *El Quijote* translations, then in France, Italy, and England. The individual as loner in touch with his own subjectivity and in communion with the cosmos is the mantra of *Sturm und Drang*, the aesthetic drive that took shape in Europe between 1760 and 1780 but had a lasting influence at least until the early part of the twentieth century, if not up to our own day. Johann Wolfgang von Goethe's *Wilhelm Meister's Apprenticeship* (1795–96), about a hero's journey of self-realization, is seen as its apogee, as is his play *Faust* (1808). Goethe, a true polyglot, knew Latin, Greek, and Italian, and was interested in Yiddish and learned Hebrew, but he was only superficially acquainted with Spanish. Still, he was a huge fan of Calderón de la Barca's plays and, to a lesser extent, of *El Quijote*. Parallels between Don Quixote and Sancho Panza and Faust and Mephistopheles are supported by the letters in which Goethe wrote that he reread *El Quijote*. The apocryphal sentence mistakenly attributed to Cervantes's novel—"*Ladran, Sancho, señal que cabalgamos*," They are barking, Sancho, proof that we're still riding forward—actually comes from Goethe's *Kläffer* (1808).

The Romantic adoration of *El Quijote* is best exemplified in France in the form of engravings of printmaker, illustrator, and sculptor Gustave Doré, who illustrated—with woodcuts and steel engravings—Louis Viardot's 1863 French translation. (Viardot prepared himself for the task of translating by reading the entire oeuvre of Montaigne, believing it shared with Cervantes's work a questioning way of approaching the world.) With the exception of the minimalist drawing by Pablo Picasso, no illustrations of this most celebrated knight-errant have been more frequently reproduced. Needless to say, these aren't the only images frequently accompanying *El Quijote*. Other celebrated artists include the nineteenth-century French caricaturist Honoré Daumier, who produced dozens of images, although he never illustrated the whole book, and the Spanish surrealist Salvador

Don Quixote and the Windmills *(1945), by Salvador Dalí.*

Dalí, who made twenty-eight drawings and ten watercolors in 1945 to illustrate the First Part of *El Quijote*, published by Random House, and then added to this production twelve lithographs he made for the Parisian edition of *Pages choises de Don Quichotte de la Mancha*, published by Joseph Foret in 1957. Dalí preferred to draw the knight-errant alone—that is, isolated, as is typical of the surrealist painter—rather than accompanied by his squire. (By the way, Dalí believed in the fanciful idea that he was a descendant of Dalí Mami, a Greek corsair to whom Cervantes was assigned as a slave during his imprisonment in Algiers.)

Yet Doré remains the king in the landscape of Quixote-inspired art. He viewed Cervantes's protagonist as *un roman-*

tique, an outsider, a genius retreating from society, in touch with his inner energy, in tune with nature, and inspired by supernatural forces. The most popular among all the artists ever to illuminate the novel, Doré published his illustrations several years before he made engravings for the Bible (both the Hebrew and the Christian parts). The Quixote images became a huge success and defined his oeuvre, which would come to include Rabelais's *Gargantua and Pantagruel* (1854), Dante's *Divine Comedy* (1857, 1866, and 1867), Shakespeare's *Tempest* (1860), and Milton's *Paradise Lost* (1866). Doré was thirty when, in 1862, he embarked on the Quixote project. He is said to have traveled to Spain, although, if one studies the lithographs closely, there seems to be little indication that the sojourn defined his aesthetic vision. The artist created mythical universes in which every single scene looks as though it was the last image of a sinking, ghostlike universe.

Doré made 113 illustrations for *El Quijote*: 57 for the First Part and 56 for the Second Part. He included approximately one drawing per chapter, although there are chapters without

Sancho Panza (1864), *by Gustave Doré.*

images and some with five. Some illustrations are more finished than others and more complex too. He signed each one with a short "G Doré" in the lower left corner. The perspective in these pictures is always shifting. When Don Quixote is captured and put in a cage, we are inside with him. When looking at the famous episode of Master Pedro's puppet show, we are part of the stage while the knight-errant, his squire, and others look on. The knight-errant's silhouette is near or far, depend-

Don Quixote and Windmills (1864), *by Gustave Doré.*

ing on the scene. When a beaten Don Quixote is in bed, his face and ours almost touch. But when he's dying, toward the end, we see him at some distance; his entourage, made of more than half-a-dozen friends and acquaintances about to begin the process of mourning, take up more physical space than he does.

Unquestionably one of the most celebrated of Doré's images presents the knight-errant in the act of fighting against the windmills. It comes in the First Part, chapter XIV, and is strategically placed after Grisóstomo's song and before the actual narrative continuing the pastoral tale of the peasant Marcela. It shows Don Quixote in midair, being struck by one of the blades, with Rocinante jumping in shock, Sancho and his donkey at a distance, and a row of windmills extending, in decreasing size, from the middle left side into the back. This engraving, whenever I come across it, simultaneously bewilders and disappoints me.

Doré, in my opinion, is not only too blunt but also too realistic. Shouldn't the windmills at least resemble giants? Shouldn't we be invited to distort reality along with Don Quixote? Who is doing the looking here? The squire? We, the viewers? The allure of El Quijote is that to its protagonist, reality isn't what the rest of us make of it. Shouldn't Doré have tried to convey in graphic terms the conflicting perspectives? There is, on the other hand, enormous energy in the image. The blade itself looks shattered, precarious, a sight that makes us think less of refined technology (that, after all, is what Don Quixote is fighting: progress) than of makeshift advancement. As usual in Doré, the sky is cloudy, threatening even. Meanwhile, Sancho, near his honking donkey, is scandalized.

The other famous Doré illustration—my favorite, reproduced as the frontispiece to this book—depicts Alonso Quijano in his room in the act of becoming Don Quixote. Quijano is dressed as a hidalgo. Balding, he wears a mustache and beard. His oblong face projects an expression of pomposity. He sits on an armchair right at the center of the engraving, his left hand holding a book, the right one raised with a sword. Around him there are books big and small, opened and closed, in piles on the floor and on a table nearby. Also surrounding him, or perhaps emerging from his imagination, are all sorts of knights and other personages riding horses or fighting dragons, giants, and other monsters of various sizes. In the monsters' midst, on both sides of Quijano, are innocent damsels caught in difficult situations: one is physically dragged from behind, the other is a prisoner begging for her life. There are even mice on the floor, on top of which are mini-knights-errant.

Not surprisingly, Doré's obsession with myth, reminiscent of the art of another Romantic printmaker, the English poet William Blake, has at times turned him into a target of derision. Even as he became one of France's most successful engravers, during his lifetime the artistic establishment looked down on him as a mere book illustrator. That ridicule hasn't ceased. In spite of their unquestionable beauty, his Quixote lithographs are often lampooned in pop culture for their melodramatic nature.

The ebullient bunch also includes an abundance of musicians. Another German admirer and a late Romantic was Richard Strauss, who in 1897 composed *Phantastische Variationen über ein Thema ritterlichen Charakters* (Fantastic Variations on a Theme of Knightly Character), Opus 35. There is also Georg Philipp Telemann's opera *Don Quichotte auf der Hochzeit des*

Camacho (1761), as well as Manuel de Falla's *El retablo de maese Pedro* (1922), a puppet-opera in one act, and the three songs for voice and piano by Maurice Ravel, collectively known as *Don Quichotte à Dulcinée* (the first one composed in 1932), set to poems by French poet, playwright, and diplomat Paul Morand. In these works, the Romantic composers portrayed the knight as a temperamental spirit uniquely in touch with his emotions, synchronized with the mood of nature as a whole, a genius whose erratic behavior is a model of inspiration and a lesson for humanity on how to appreciate life to its fullest.

In total, there are seven full ballets based on *El Quijote*, all of them forgettable. The most famous is French choreographer Marius Petipa's version, first staged by the Bolshoi in Moscow in 1869 to the music of Austrian composer and violin virtuoso Ludwig Minkus. Interestingly, this was one of the only ballets not expurgated from the Bolshoi repertoire after the Bolshevik Revolution in 1917, probably because the protagonist was perceived by the newly empowered proletarian elite as representing a refutation of bourgeois society. Its structure is rather simplistic: At the beginning, Don Quixote is in his study, dreaming of Dulcinea. As he falls asleep, Sancho shows up. The knight-errant tells him about the adventure he is about to embark on. The action then moves to a Barcelona marketplace, even though Barcelona does not appear in the original story until the end. At one point they are in a gypsy camp. There is an episode with Master Pedro's puppet show, although modern versions eliminate it. Petipa's ballet isn't interested in verisimilitude. The only objective is to place the knight-errant in circumstances in which he refuses to fit into society, opting to be an idealist.

In contrast with ballet, the field of opera has been more fertile. There are around twenty operas based on *El Quijote*. One is by the nineteenth-century Austrian composer Wilhelm Kienzl. It was completed in 1897 to celebrate the 350th anniversary of Cervantes's birth, and it premiered a year later in Berlin's Neues Königliches Opernhaus. Jules Massenet wrote another one, *Don Quichotte*, which uses a libretto of Henri Caïn. Based on the play *Le chevalier de la longue figure*, by poet Jacques Le Lorrain, it was first performed in 1904. Made of five acts, this one has a rather loose, disjointed structure. This is aside from the extemporaneous elements it introduces. In truth, the Massenet opera is interested only in the Don Quixote–Dulcinea relationship—and it is sheer melodrama. At one point, the knight-errant watches as four handsome males court her. To gain her favor, he must fight a cadre of giants as well as a bandit named Ténébrun. When Don Quixote finally tells Dulcinea he loves her, she replies with a rather saccharine line: "*je souffre votre tristesse*," I suffer your sadness.

Filmmakers have been particularly drawn to *El Quijote*. In most cases, however, their efforts have resulted in disaster. I frequently ask myself why. It sometimes looks as if there is a curse, as one moviemaking effort after another falls apart before reaching the big screen, or is released to resounding disappointment. Or it may be plain bad luck. German director Werner Herzog toyed with the idea for a while, but he never completed a movie version. Yet several of his movies are about unrealistic, impractical individuals, or about individuals limited by their environment, and, as such, they are effusively quixotic. Take the case of *Aguirre, the Wrath of God* (1972), about Spanish conquistador Lope de Aguirre looking for gold in the

Amazon. Or else *Fitzcarraldo* (1982), which is about a deranged Irish rubber baron who decided to pull a steamship over a hill in Peru. Even Herzog's documentaries *Grizzly Man* (2005), about the bear lover Timothy Treadwell, who ended up being devoured by bears in Alaska, and *Cave of Forgotten Dreams* (2010), about the Chauvet Cave in southern France, are dreamy in nature.

Examples of complete adaptations of Cervantes's novel populate almost every national cinematic tradition. There are Russian versions (e.g., *Don Kikhot* [1961], directed by Grigori Kozintsev) as well as French ones (e.g., a short by the excellent director Éric Rohmer, called *Don Quichotte de Cervantes* [1965]), and a handful, either shorts or feature films, from Portugal, Hungary, Italy, Greece, and South Africa, to name a few countries. Peter Yates, in 2000, did an infelicitous TV movie with John Lithgow, Bob Hoskins, and Isabella Rossellini. A children's animated adaptation, *Donkey Xote* (2007), directed by José Pozo (who is also responsible for a cartoon version of *El Cid*), tells the story from the perspective of Rucio, Sancho's donkey (who wants to be a horse), and presents the argument that the knight-errant isn't a lunatic but a wise, passionate man.

And, of course, there are plenty of Spanish versions, among them Manuel Gutiérrez Aragón's unbearably boring two-part film made for television: the segment based on the First Part was done in 1991, the one on the Second Part in 2002. The overall effect of these screen efforts is numbing: the right habitat for *El Quijote*, it seems, isn't the moving image. Film tends to constrain Cervantes's imagination, to make it pedestrian. In literature, the reader's imagination flies because it is free to alternate between the real and the fantastical, between what the knight-errant sees and what others want him to visualize.

I have written about the Cantinflas versions, undoubtedly the most popular. But in the late twentieth century and the beginning of the twenty-first, especially in the Spanish-speaking world, people also have access to *El Quijote* by other means: video games. During a period known as the Golden Age of the Spanish *videojuego*, *Don Quijote* (1987) had versions in ZX Spectrum, Amstrad CPC, Commodore 64, MSX, Atari ST, and DOS. Other, more sophisticated Quixote-inspired video games included one in which he and El Cid fight zombies, yet this one caught the attention of the largest number of players. The game was divided into two parts. In the first one, Don Quixote needed to become a knight-errant, complete with his shining armor, in order to start his adventures. And in the second part, he needed to look for the ingredients of the *Bálsamo de Fierabrás* because, after suffering an accident, the elixir would be able to heal him so he could reunite with his beloved Dulcinea. It might be worth adding that while there are other video games based on classic literature (from Dante's *Inferno* and Bradbury's *Fahrenheit 451* to Salinger's *Catcher in the Rye* and Fitzgerald's *Great Gatsby*, not to mention the Bible), this, to my knowledge, is the only one based on a Spanish-language novel.

Despite the many artistic, musical, and technological adaptations of *El Quijote*, it is in literature where the biggest, most commanding fans of the novel are to be found. José Ortega y Gasset said, in *Meditations on Quijote*, that Emma Bovary is *"un Don Quijote con faldas y un mínimo de tragedia sobre el alma,"* a Don Quixote in skirts and a minimum of tragedy over the soul. The resemblance is clear from the novel's plotline: Living a placid, countryside life near the town of Rouen in Normandy, Emma Bovary, the heroine of Flaubert's 1856 novel, is a reader bored out of her wits. She reads in order to escape the reality that surrounds her. She is unhappy with her husband, Charles, a mediocre doctor. Her diet includes romances, women's magazines, historic romances, and the novels of Eugène Sue, Balzac, and George Sand. So as to inject passion into her days, she engages in an affair with a landowner, Rodolphe Boulanger. The affair undergoes a series of ups and downs, passing through periods of intensity but ending in a breakup. She starts another affair with a lawyer, Léon Dupuis. Eventually he grows tired of her. At that point she begins buying luxury items on credit. The collapse of the affair and her monetary ruin drive her to commit suicide.

El Quijote transformed Flaubert when he first read it during his adolescent years. In a letter of 1832, written when he was still eleven years old, he says he's making notes on the novel. A couple of decades later and four years before he published *Madame Bovary*, he told poet Louise Colet, with whom he engaged in an affair, "What is characteristic of great geniuses are their faculty of generalizing and their power of creation. They create types, each of which epitomizes a class, and by doing so they enrich the consciousness of mankind. Don't we believe that *Don Quixote* is as real as Caesar?" By way of comparison, he added, "Shakespeare is formidable in this regard. He was not a man, he was a continent: he contained whole crowds of great men, entire landscapes." A few weeks later, still in 1852, he told Colet that great books have a special quality: the more one contemplates them, the bigger they grow: "What is prodigious about *Don Quixote*," Flaubert stated, "is the absence of art, and that perpetual fusion of illusion and reality which makes the book so comic and so poetic. All others are such dwarfs beside it!"

When around 1863 Flaubert corresponded with his friend Ivan Turgenev, he told him that *El Quijote* makes him "long to ride a horse along a road white with dust and eat olives and raw onions in the shade of a rock." This passion never diminished. In a letter to George Sand dated some six years later, he mentioned he was rereading the Cervantes novel. "What a giant of a book! Is there anything more splendid?" But his most impressive assessments came as he declared his roots as a novelist: "*Je retrouve mes origines dans le livre que je savais par coeur avant de savoir lire, Don Quichotte*," I rediscovered my origins in the book I knew by heart before knowing how to read, *Don Quixote*. In other words, Flaubert made *El Quijote* his own before he even read the book.

Yet what exactly does it mean "to make it one's own"? How is Emma "a knight in skirts"? The commonalities are obvious: an existential disaffection, a refusal to follow social conventions, a rebellious spirit, and the compulsion to battle with one's own demons. The real question is what differentiates the knight-errant from the rural housewife. The response might be plentiful (one is Spanish and the other French, this one is moneyless and thus belongs to a feudal culture while the other springs from a bourgeois environment and uses credit to enhance her delusions, etc.), but the basic divergence is that one is a man, the other a woman.

Flaubert once famously said, "Madame Bovary *c'est moi*." Comparing Cervantes and Flaubert with their protagonists is thought-provoking. Is it more difficult for a male writer to create a female character than to produce one of his own gender?

(The argument might also be made that female writers actually write male characters very well, because they observe them so closely, needing to anticipate their behavior, or perhaps for safety or survival.) Think of how few novelists are successful in this transgender odyssey: Henry James, E. M. Forster, and Naguib Mahfouz, but not Italo Calvino, Philip Roth, and Vargas Llosa. Actually, in *El Quijote* itself, the female characters, although abundant in number, are relatively minor: Dulcinea, Marcela, Dorothea, Leonor, Maritornes, Altisidora, Teresa Panza, Sanchita, Princess Micomicona, Zenaida, the Duchess, Alonso Quijano's niece and housekeeper, among others. (Cervantes was married in 1584, at the age of thirty-seven, to nineteen-year-old Catalina de Salazar. But he had an out-of-wedlock daughter with another nineteen-year-old, the result of a night of passion at a tavern.) In contrast, Flaubert delves into his novel with a genuinely female viewpoint. This, in my estimation, is a truly quixotic achievement.

As for Dostoyevsky, his route to *El Quijote* is somewhat different. He heard Ivan Turgenev lecture in 1860 on the similarities and differences between Hamlet and Don Quixote. The lecture in Russian was titled "*Gamet I Don-Kikhot.*" In Turgenev's view, Shakespeare's prince is a man of reason, doubt, egotism, and skepticism, whereas Quixote is a man of belief, faith, devotion, and sacrifice. Turgenev thought that human psychology oscillated between these two poles, and he identified with Don Quixote. Dostoyevsky reacted with wonderment. He too identified with the knight-errant, whom he saw as a variation of Jesus Christ. He decided to turn that wonderment into literature, first—and loosely—in Raskolnikov, the protagonist of *Crime and Punishment* (1866), then—emphatically—in *The Idiot* (1869), where the protagonist, Prince Myshkin, an outright variation on Don Quixote, symbolizes the most optimistic, benevolent, perhaps even naive aspects of human nature. In a letter to his niece Sophia Ivanova, written in Geneva on January 13, 1868, about the idea for a new novel, Dostoyevsky wrote:

> There is only one positively beautiful person in the world, Christ, and the phenomenon of this limitlessly, infinitely beautiful person is an infinite miracle in itself. (The whole Gospel according to John is about that: for him the whole miracle is only in the incarnation, in the manifestation of the beautiful.) But I am going too far. I'd only mention that of all the beautiful individuals in Christian literature, one stands out as the most perfect, Don Quixote. But he is beautiful only because he is ridiculous.

Clearly, Dostoyevsky mixed his literary admiration with religious undertones. He once wrote in his diaries that "in the whole world there is no deeper, no mightier literary work. This is, so far, the last and greatest expression of human thought; this is the bitterest irony which man was capable of conceiving. And if the world were to come to an end, and people were asked there, somewhere: 'did you understand your life on earth, and what conclusion have you drawn from it?'—man could silently hand over *Don Quixote*: 'Such is my inference from life. Can you condemn me for it?' "

Elsewhere, Dostoyevsky admires Don Quixote's capacity to believe in the unbelievable, to appreciate the irrational aspects of life. In September 1877, he elaborated on this theory in his personal diary. Although this is a long quote, it is worth looking at his meditation in full (in Kenneth Lantz's translation):

Oh, this is a great book, not the sort that are written now; only one such book is sent to humanity in several hundred years. And such perceptions of the profoundest aspects of human nature you will find in every page of this book. Take only the fact that this Sancho, the personification of common sense, prudence, cunning, the golden mean, has chanced to become a friend and traveling companion of the maddest person on earth—he precisely, and no other! He deceives him the whole time, he cheats him like a child, and yet he has complete faith in his great intellect, is enchanted to the point of tenderness of the greatness of his heart, believes completely in all the preposterous dreams of the great knight, and the whole time he never once doubts that the Don will at last conquer the island for him! What a fine thing it would be if our young people were to become thoroughly steeped in these great works of world literature. I don't know what is now being taught in courses of literature, but a knowledge of this most splendid and sad of all books created by human genius would certainly elevate the soul of a young person with a great idea, give rise to profound questions in the heart, and work toward diverting his mind from worship of the eternal and foolish idol of mediocrity, self-satisfied conceit, and cheap prudence. Man will not forget to take this *saddest* of all books with him to God's last judgment. He will point to the most profound and fateful mystery of humans and humankind that the book conveys. He will point to the fact that humanity's most sublime beauty, its most sublime purity, chastity, forthrightness, gentleness, courage, and, finally, its most sublime intellect—all these often (alas, all too often) come to naught, pass without benefit to humanity, and even become an object of humanity's derision simply because all these most noble and precious gifts with which a person is often endowed lack but the very last gift—that of *genius* to put all this power to work and to direct it along a path of action that is truthful, not fantastic or insane, so as to work for the benefit of humanity! But genius, alas, is given out to the tribes and the people in such small quantities and so rarely that the spectacle of the malicious irony of fate that so often dooms the efforts of some of the noblest of people and the most ardent friends of humanity to scorn and laughter and to the casting of stones solely because these people, at the fateful moment, were unable to discern the true sense of things and so discover their *new word*—this spectacle of the needless ruination of such great and noble forces actually may reduce a friend of humanity to despair, evoke not laughter but bitter tears and sour the heart, hitherto pure and believing, with doubt. . . .

However, I wanted only to point out this most interesting feature which, along with hundreds of other such profound perceptions, Cervantes revealed in the human heart. The most preposterous of people, with a crackpot belief in the most preposterous fantasy anyone can conceive, suddenly falls into doubt and perplexity that almost shake his entire faith. . . . The preposterous man suddenly *began yearning for realism*! It wasn't the appearance of sorcerers' armies that bothered him: oh, that's beyond any doubt; and how else could these great and splendid knights display all their valor if they were not visited by all these trials, if there were no envious giants and wicked sorcerers? The ideal of the wandering knight is so great, so beautiful and useful, and had so captivated the heart of the noble Don Quixote that it became utterly impossible for him to renounce his faith in it; that would have been the equivalent of betraying his ideal, his duty, his love for Dulcinea and for humanity. (When he did renounce his ideal, when he was cured of his madness and grew *wiser*, after returning from his second campaign in which he was defeated by the wise and commonsensical barber Carrasco, the skeptic and debunker, he promptly passed away, quietly, with a sad smile, consoling the weeping Sancho, loving the whole world with the mighty force of love contained in his sacred heart, and yet realizing that there was nothing more for him to do in this world.) No, it was not that: what troubled him was merely the very real, mathematical consideration that no matter how the knight might wield his word and no matter how strong he might be, he still could not overcome an army of a hundred thousand in the course of a few hours, or even in a day, having killed all of them to the last man. And yet such things were written in these trustworthy books. Therefore, they must have lied. And if there is one lie, then it is all a lie. How, then, can *truth* be saved? And so, to save the truth he invents another fantasy; but this one is twice, thrice as fantastic as the first one, cruder and more absurd: he invents hundreds of thousands of imaginary men having the bodies of slugs, which the knight's keen blade can pass through ten times more easily and quickly than it can an ordinary human body. And thus *realism* is satisfied, *truth* is saved, and it's possible to believe in the first and most important dream with no more doubts—and all this, again, is solely thanks to the second, even more absurd fantasy, invented only to salvage the *realism* of the first one.

Ask yourselves: hasn't the same thing happened to you, perhaps, a hundred times in the course of your life? Say you've come to cherish a certain dream, an idea, a theory, a conviction, or some eternal fact that struck you, or, at least, a woman who has enchanted you. You rush off in pursuit of the object of your love with all the intensity your soul can muster. It's true that no matter how blinded you may be, no matter how well your heart bribes you, still, if in the object of your love there is a lie, a *delusion*, something that you yourself have exaggerated and distorted because of your passion and your initial rush of feeling—solely so that you can make it your idol and bow down to it—then, of course, you're aware of it in the depth of your being; doubt weighs upon your mind and teases it, ranges through your soul and prevents you from living peaceably with your beloved dream. Now, don't you remember, won't you admit even to yourself what it was that suddenly set your mind at rest? Didn't you invent a new dream, a new lie, even a terribly crude one, perhaps, but one that you were quick to embrace lovingly only because it resolved your initial doubt?

The *saddest* book . . . While Miguel de Unamuno approached Don Quixote as a religious figure who helped us to see what was simple and authentic in a world that is a prisoner of deception (a connection that was used to explain the Spanish national character), Dostoyevsky's faith was less nationalistic, sadder, and more raw. He saw *El Quijote* as the novel that explored the realm of our dreams. For him it was a book that went against institutionalized faith.

Interestingly, another Russian, Vladimir Nabokov, believed *El Quijote* was the cruelest of all novels. In a series of lectures delivered at Harvard in 1951–52, published posthumously in 1983, Nabokov wrote, "That in former times a reader could get a belly-laugh from every chapter of the work, seems incredible to the modern reader, who finds the implication of its humor brutal and grim." He added, "The fun often sinks to the low level of the medieval farce with all its conventional laughing-stocks. It is sad when an author assumes that certain things are funny in themselves—donkeys, gluttons, tormented animals, bloody noses, et cetera—to stock in trade of ready-made fun." Nabokov also disliked *The Brothers Karamazov* (which, he noted with pleasure, in some English editions was called "The Kalamazoo Brothers") and thought *Crime and Punishment* to be a ghastly rigmarole ("No, I do not object to soul-searching and self-revelation," he added, "but in those books the soul, and the sins, and the sentimentality, and the journalese, hardly warrant the tedious and muddled search"). About Cervantes's novel, he wrote:

It is simply not true that as some of our mellow-minded commentators maintain—Aubrey Bell, for instance—

that the general character that emerges from the national background of the book is that of sensitive, keen-witted folks, humorous and humane. Humane, indeed! What about the hideous cruelty—with or without the author's intent or sanction—which riddles the whole book and befouls its humor? Let us not drag the national element in. The Spaniards of Don Quixote's day were not more cruel in their behavior toward madmen and animals, subordinates and non-conformers, than any other nation of that brutal and brilliant era. Or, for that matter, of other, later, more brutal and less brilliant eras in which the fact of cruelty remains with its fangs bared.

El Quijote is, Nabokov says, "one of the most bitter and barbarous books ever penned." He argues that in the novel everyone deceives everyone else and all make fun of Alonso Quijano/ Don Quixote. They abuse animals, beat slaves, attack defenseless people, and stage plays with no other purpose than to insult, exploit, manipulate, and mistreat.

It is interesting to contrast these two Russians, Dostoyevsky and Nabokov. The first is passionate; the second brainy. One likes effusive, episodic novels; the other despises them. (For Nabokov, El Quijote was a "one-and-a-half track" novel, whereas Madame Bovary was a one-track narrative and Anna Karenina, which he spells Karenin, a multi-track.) One believes the novel to be a great work of world literature; the other finds its value over-hyped. Nabokov once stated, "Some critics, a very vague minority long dead, have tried to prove that Don Quixote is but a stale farce. Others have maintained that Don Quixote is the greatest novel ever written. A hundred years ago one enthusiastic French critic, Charles-Augustin Sainte-Beuve, author of *Les Lundis* (1851–1872), called it 'the Bible of Humanity.' Let us not fall under the spell of such enchanters." Nabokov also declared that **"***Don Quixote* is one of those books that are, perhaps, more important in eccentric diffusion than in their own intrinsic value." He recommended that we "do our best to avoid the fatal error of looking for so-called 'real life' in novels." He added, "Let us not try and reconcile the fiction of facts with the facts of fiction. *Don Quixote* is a fairy tale, so is *Bleak House*, so is *Dead Souls*. *Madame Bovary* and *Anna Karenin* are supreme fairy tales. But without these fairy tales the world would not be real."

I like Nabokov's last point. Despite his aversion to *El Quijote*, he is sure the world would "not be real" without it, because in the end, fairy tales such as the one Cervantes gave us show that life isn't what the eye can see but what our imagination makes with the raw material that surrounds us.

Another distinguished member of the ebullient bunch is Franz Kafka. With him, the Cervantes novel curiously enters a mystical realm. When Kafka died at the age of forty-one, among his manuscripts were found a series of unpublished parables, secular variations of the Hasidic tradition, in which a tale is retold to showcase the mechanics, irremediably mysterious, through which God rules the world. *"Die Wahrheit über Sancho Panza,"* or "The Truth about Sancho Panza," proposes a different way of looking at Cervantes's novel. The English translation by Willa and Edwin Muir reads:

> Without making any boast of it, Sancho Panza succeeded in the course of years, by feeding him a great

number of romances of chivalry and adventure in the evening and night hours, in so diverting from himself his demon, whom he later called Don Quixote, that this demon thereupon set out, uninhibited, on the maddest exploits, which, however, for the lack of a preordained object, which should have been Sancho Panza himself, harmed nobody. A free man, Sancho Panza philosophically followed Don Quixote on his crusades, perhaps out of a sense of responsibility, and had of them a great and edifying entertainment to the end of his days.

From the title onward, Kafka suggests that readers up until now have failed to understand the *actual* place the squire plays in Cervantes's novel: he is not just a servant; his responsibility is far greater. Sancho, Kafka announces, does not play the role of supporting cast, as we've been led to believe; instead, he is the lead protagonist, even more important than his master. A modest man (he does not "boast about" his own achievements), he is inhabited by a demon (the word in German is *dämon*, evil spirit). To free himself from it, he begets Don Quixote, to whom Sancho patiently feeds "a great number of romances of chivalry and adventure in the evening and night hours." That way he manages to "divert the demon" from himself.

In Hasidism, an imprisoned demon seeking to emerge is called a *dybbuk*. But this demon is generally understood to have come from the outside, to have sought refuge in a person's body in order to right a wrong. But in "The Truth about Sancho Panza," Kafka's imagery is more subtle. The demon is not an outsider. It might not even represent a negative attribute. Instead, Sancho's demon might be a metaphor for an artist freeing himself from his personal hang-ups through invention. Still, the squire's creation of Don Quixote requires a kind of exorcism. Allowing the demon out makes Sancho a free man. But it does not liberate him altogether. Rather, that liberation entails other types of submission: first, because Sancho becomes his master's servant, dutifully following Don Quixote ("out of a sense of responsibility"), and is rewarded with merriment ("a great and edifying entertainment to the end of his days"); and second, because he is bound to chivalry literature, using it as a sort of alchemy to form the figure of Don Quixote.

Kafka upsets the Don Quixote–Sancho equation, turning the relationship upside down. The parable makes the knight-errant a figment of the squire's imagination. The master is a master not only because he has a servant—the master is the servant's creation. The servant's genius lies not in begetting a creation in which he is on top, but by remaining at the bottom where his power is deeper. In Kafka's view, the ruled are actually in control of the rulers.

Walter Benjamin, who was fascinated with mysticism and befriended the Jewish scholar Gershom Scholem, the author of *Kabbalah* (1974), sums it up accurately: "It is highly revealing that Kafka was able to recognize (though unable to create) the figure of the supremely religious man, a man who is in the right. And where did he find him? In none other than Sancho Panza, who has freed himself from a promiscuous relationship with his demon by directing the demon toward another object than himself, so that he might pursue a peaceful life in which he has no need to forget anything." To be sure, Kafka argues symbolically that freedom, as such, is impossible. He once outlined a sequel in which the knight-errant was scheduled to visit southern France and northern Italy. Fittingly for Kafka, who might be called "the master of defeat," the enterprise came to nothing.

As for Borges, his own parable in the form of "Pierre Menard" is not his only writing on the novel. He also wrote poems, protests, and a dream inspired by *El Quijote*. In January 1955, he wrote "*Parábola de Cervantes y el Quijote*," collected in his book *El hacedor* (1960). Sancho does not play a role in this parable. Instead, Borges imagines a dialectical relationship between Cervantes and Don Quixote. At first, these two entities are clearly defined. But time attenuates their differences until creator and creation become one and the same. This is my English translation:

> Tired of his land in Spain, one of the king's old soldiers sought solace in Ariosto's vast geographies, in that valley of the moon where the time wasted by dreams is found and in Mohammed's golden idol stolen by Montalbán.
>
> In gentle mockery of himself, he devised a credulous man who, perturbed by his reading of marvels, gave in to searching prowess and enchantments in prosaic places called El Toboso and Montiel.
>
> Defeated by reality, by Spain, Don Quixote died in his native village around 1614. He was survived but for a short time by Miguel de Cervantes.
>
> For both of them, the dreamer and the dreamed one, this whole plot resulted from the opposition of two worlds: the unreal world of chivalry novels and the quotidian, common world of the seventeenth century.

They never suspected that the years would end up smoothing away their discord; they didn't suspect that La Mancha and Montiel and the knight's lean figure would be, for the future, no less poetic than Sinbad's episodes or Ariosto's vast geographies.

For in the beginning of literature is myth, and in the end too.

9

AMERICA'S
EXCEPTIONALISM

eorge Washington purchased a copy of *El Quijote* in Philadelphia on the very day the Constitution was adopted, September 17, 1787. It was the four-volume Tobias Smollett translation, which cost him, in Pennsylvania currency, twenty-two shillings, six pence. His presidential library at Mount Vernon still holds it, with Washington's signature on the title page of each volume as well as an impression of his bookplate in the front paste-down endpaper. Earlier that same year, Washington had engaged in correspondence with Don Diego de Gardoqui, Spain's ambassador. The topic was trade along the Mississippi River, which would be beneficial to Spain. On September 11, Gardoqui visited the future first president, and the conversation included the topic of Cervantes. Almost a couple of months later, the Spanish ambassador wrote to Washington, "requesting you would accept, and give a place in your library, to the best Spanish edition of Don Quixote [a copy published in Madrid in 1780]."

When Washington died in 1799, the eighteen-page inventory of his books described the English "Donquixote" as being "On the Table." Its value then was assessed at three dollars.

El Quijote was one of Jefferson's favorites, as many references to it in his letters attest. Benjamin Franklin owned a five-volume Spanish edition, which he prized as an outstanding example of the typographer's art. He used the novel to teach himself Spanish and encouraged his children to do the same. In his correspondence, full of adulation for the book, he described himself also as "combat[ing] against windmills." In addition, Franklin noted that while "Don Quixote undertook to redress the bodily wrongs of the world," he, Franklin, recognized that the "redressment of mental vagaries" in the United States around 1822 "would be an enterprise more than Quixotic." Still, he used Cervantes's template to plow forward with a plan to make America "the Canaan of the New World."

If the Spanish-speaking Americas have fostered an aesthetic philosophy called *Menardismo* that has been liberating in its capacity to cultivate a postcolonial mentality, in the United States, *El Quijote* is read altogether differently: as a guidebook to exceptionalism. A profusion of English translations, five in the eighteenth century and four in the nineteenth, all of them produced in England (none would be published in America until the mid-twentieth century), made *El Quijote* ever popular on these shores.

The Founding Fathers were not the only devotees in the early Republic. Motifs and characters in *El Quijote* show up frequently in the realm of letters. Hugh Henry Brackenridge, an early American judge and writer, published a satirical novel, *Modern Chivalry: Containing the Adventures of Captain John Farrago and Teague O'Regan, His servant*, set on a western Pennsylvania farm, yet borrowing much from Cervantes's book. Its protagonist, Captain John Farrago, sets out "to write about the world a little, with his man Teague at his heels, to see how things were going on here and there, and to observe human nature." The first two parts appeared in 1792, the third in 1793, and the fourth in 1797, with a revised version in 1805. John Adams said Brackenridge's book was "a more thoroughly American book than any written before 1833." Equally significant is Tabitha Gilman Tenney's novel *Female Quixotism, Exhibited in the Romantic Opinions and Extravagant Adventures of Dorcasina Sheldon*, released in 1801, a quarter of a century after the country became independent. A critique of romantic literature, this hilarious book, only loosely related to *El Quijote*, is a cautionary tale about the extent to which young ladies might damage their character by reading novels. It was the most popular novel in the United States before Harriet Beecher Stowe's *Uncle Tom's Cabin*. Both Brackenridge and Tenney saw Cervantes's protagonist as the ancestor of the frontier American.

The Founding Fathers, in their eighteenth-century quest for a nation where everyone would be entitled to a decent life, where liberty and the pursuit of happiness would be the central tenets, saw in Cervantes's hero an ideal. The belief that the United States needed to be a bastion of tolerance and individualism, a place where people would be free to engage in quests of the imagination, led these political leaders to embrace Don Quixote as their own advisor.

The nineteenth-century United States turned Don Quixote

and his creator, Cervantes, into paragons of individualism, especially in New England. William Cullen Bryant, the romantic poet and longtime editor of the *New York Evening Post*, wrote a poem about "The Prince of Wits" in an April 23, 1878, edition commemorating the anniversary of Cervantes's death. This is the opening statement:

> As o'er the laughter-moving page
> Thy readers, oh, Cervantes, bend,
> What shouts of mirth, through age on age,
> From every clime of earth ascend!

Bryant saw Don Quixote as an exemplar of human folly. He saw readers "honoring thee" in fighting the "shadow of a coming night." Don Quixote's struggle was that of dreams the world over.

As the concept of "Manifest Destiny" became ingrained in the American mentality to justify the large territorial expansion toward the west (some of it involving the conquest of territories of Spain and Mexico), intellectuals, principally in New England but also in Texas and California, began to ardently admire Don Quixote for his bravery in embarking on a quest into the great unknown. His fans included Washington Irving and Nathaniel Hawthorne, Stephen Crane and William Dean Howells.

Washington Irving, a Hispanophile who authored *A History of the Life and Voyages of Christopher Columbus* (1828) and served as minister to Spain under President John Tyler, was deeply influenced by the book. He frequently refers to *El Quijote* in his work. At one point in his *History of New York* (1809), told through the invented persona of Diedrich Knickerbocker, he described Peter Stuyvesant, a major figure in early New York history, as "a man who studied for years in the chivalrous library of Don Quixote." And in *Tales of the Alhambra* (1832) there are ongoing references to the knight-errant's madness as a key to understanding the Spanish psyche.

But the greatest American tribute paid to *El Quijote* is also by one of the greatest nineteenth-century American novelists: Herman Melville. Melville called Don Quixote "the greatest sage that ever lived." Traces of Cervantes are present throughout his oeuvre, for instance, in *White Jacket; or, The World in a Man-of-War* (1850), where one of the shipmates reads *Don Quixote*. And *The Confidence-Man* (1857), which Melville wrote while reading that book himself, includes a character similar to Cide Hamete Benengeli. Melville even wrote a poem, dated somewhere around 1870–76, about a lifetime of rereading Cervantes's novel:

"THE RUSTY MAN"
BY A SOURED ONE

In La Mancha he mopeth,
    With beard thin and dusty;
He doteth and mopeth
    In Library fusty –
'Mong his old folios gropeth:

Cites obsolete saws –
Of chivalry's laws –
Be the wronged one's knight:
Die, but do right.
So he rusts and musts,
While each grocer green
Thriveth apace with the fulsome face
Of a fool serene.

Melville's great novel (maybe the greatest of all American novels), *Moby-Dick: or, The Whale* (1851), might be read as an homage to his predecessors. The hunt for the white whale mimics another impossible task: Don Quixote's battle against the forces of evil. Captain Ahab is stubborn, just like the knight-errant. His goal is to kill the white whale, just as Don Quixote's quest is to expose the enchanters. Plus, his itinerant life resembles that of Cervantes's protagonist: he travels a long, twisted path to find the meaning of his existence. The connection might even run deeper. Captain Ahab is visited by dreams. As the novel progresses, he is delusional. A couple of chapters in the novel are titled "Knights and Squires." And the character of the harpooner Queequeg has traits of Sancho. Moreover, to me this novel is really Latin American in its encyclopedic spirit.

American critic Harry Levin, in a lecture called "Don Quixote and Moby-Dick," delivered for Harvard's commemoration of the 400th anniversary of Cervantes's birth in 1946, wrote, "Where Cervantes undermines romance with realism, Melville lures us from a literal to a symbolic plane. . . . The relation of *Moby-Dick* to *Don Quixote* is neither close nor similar; it is complementary and dialectical. One proposes worldly wisdom as the touchstone for an outworn set of ideals; the other, abandoning economic values, goes questing after a transcendental faith."

Alongside Melville is another Cervantes aficionado: Mark Twain. Several of his books, including *The Prince and the Pauper* (1881), have quixotic ingredients. Twain probably read *El Quijote* when he was writing *The Innocents Abroad* (1869). He talks about Cervantes's novel in *Life on the Mississippi* (1883), preferring Cervantes to Sir Walter Scott. And *A Connecticut Yankee in King Arthur's Court* (1889) is a satire of chivalric values. But his indisputable tribute to *El Quijote* is the *Adventures of Huckleberry Finn* (1884). Establishing the centrality of this classic, Ernest Hemingway once said that "all modern American literature comes from it," hailing it as "the best book we've had."

George Santayana, a Spanish citizen who always perceived of himself as an American (he was raised in the United States and taught philosophy at Harvard), wrote an influential 1952 essay in which he connects *The Adventures of Tom Sawyer* to *El Quijote*, meditating on the extent to which Twain was in debt to Cervantes. Indeed, Tom Sawyer might be seen to be like Don Quixote: he reads books and wants life to fit into them. In chapter 3 of *Huckleberry Finn*, while he and his club are in a cave, plotting one of their ruckuses, Huck says:

> I didn't see no di'monds, and I told Tom Sawyer so. He said there was loads of them there, anyway; and he said there was Arabs there, too, and elephants and things. I said, why couldn't we see them, then? He said if I warn't

so ignorant, but had read a book called "*Don Quixote*," I would know without asking. He said it was all done by enchantment. He said there was hundreds of soldiers there, and elephants and treasure, and so on, but we had enemies which he called magicians, and they had turned the whole thing into an infant Sunday school, just out of spite. I said, allright, then the thing for us to do was to go for the magicians. Tom Sawyer said I was a numskull.

Yet the true "Cervantean" pair is made up of Huck and the runaway slave Jim. Their journey along the Mississippi River resembles that of Don Quixote and Sancho. For "Nigger Jim," their quest is suffused with the possibility of his escaping slavery in an abolitionist state, whereas the fourteen-year-old boy flees from his tyrannical father and, equally important, from an environment that limits his imagination. These two are also a rather odd couple, like Don Quixote and Sancho: short and tall, child and adult, free and enslaved, in school and unschooled, and, consequently, speaking radically different languages.

In the antebellum United States, accolades for *El Quijote* also came from Carl Schurz, the statesman and reformer (known for the saying "My country right or wrong; if right, to be kept right; and if wrong, to be set right") who served as ambassador to Spain under Lincoln. Schurtz was often depicted as a quixotic character because of "his true Americanism," even though he was born in Germany. Another enthusiast was William Dean Howells, who edited the *Atlantic Monthly* and authored *The Rise of Silas Lapham* (1885). Known as "the Dean of American Letters," in his autobiography, *My Literary Passions* (1895), Howells describes how as a child he discovered *El Quijote* when his father told the family of "a book that he had once read" about "the fevered life of the knight truly without fear and without reproach":

> I recall very fully the moment and the place when I first heard of "Don Quixote," while as yet I could not connect it very distinctly with anybody's authorship. I was still too young to conceive of authorship, even in my own case, and wrote my miserable verses without any notion of literature, or of anything but the pleasure of seeing them actually come out rightly rhymed and measured. The moment was at the close of a summer's day just before supper, which, in our house, we had lawlessly late, and the place was the kitchen where my mother was going about her work, and listening as she could to what my father was telling my brother and me and an apprentice of ours, who was like a brother to us both, of a book that he had once read. We boys were all shelling peas, but the story, as it went on, rapt us from the poor employ, and whatever our fingers were doing, our spirits were away in that strange land of adventures and mishaps, where the fevered life of the knight truly without fear and without reproach burned itself out. I dare say that my father tried to make us understand the satirical purpose of the book. I vaguely remember his speaking of the books of chivalry it was meant to ridicule; but a boy could not care for this, and what I longed to do at once was to get that book and plunge into its story. He told us at random of the attack

on the windmills and the flocks of sheep, of the night in the valley of the fulling-mills with their trip-hammers, of the inn and the muleteers, of the tossing of Sancho in the blanket, of the island that was given him to govern, and of all the merry pranks at the duke's and duchess's, of the liberation of the galley-slaves, of the capture of Mambrino's helmet, and of Sancho's invention of the enchanted Dulcinea, and whatever else there was wonderful and delightful in the most wonderful and delightful book in the world. I do not know when or where my father got it for me, and I am aware of an appreciable time that passed between my hearing of it and my having it. The event must have been most important to me, and it is strange I cannot fix the moment when the precious story came into my hands; though for the matter of that there is nothing more capricious than a child's memory, what it will hold and what it will lose.

Howell's contemporary, James Russell Lowell, the American poet, critic, and diplomat, wrote a poem in which he imagined the author of *El Quijote* in chains yet as an exemplar of freedom. In Lowell's "Prison of Cervantes," Cervantes's captivity in Algiers is a lesson about how the body might be compromised yet the mind is unbound. The poem reads in part:

> In charmed communion with his dual mind
> He wandered Spain, himself both knight and hind,
> Redressing wrongs he knew must ever be.
> His humor wise could see life's long deceit,
> Man's baffled aims, nor therefore both despise;

His knightly nature could ill fortune greet
Like an old friend.

A lifelong reader of the novel, Lowell also delivered a lecture, circa 1885, at the Working Men's College in London, in which he described this most engaging of books, comparing it to Daniel Defoe's *Robinson Crusoe* (1719). In my mind, it is among the most eloquent reflections on *El Quijote* ever produced. Here is a section from the middle:

> But *Don Quixote*, if less verisimilar as a narrative, and I am not sure that it is, appeals to far higher qualities of mind and demands a far subtler sense of appreciation than the masterpiece of Defoe. If the latter represents in simplest prose what interests us because it *might* happen to any man, the other, while seeming never to leave the low level of fact and possibility, constantly suggests the loftier region of symbol, and sets before us that eternal contrast between the ideal and the real, between the world as it might be and the world as it is, between the fervid completeness of conception and the chill inadequacy of fulfillment, which life sooner or later, directly or indirectly, forces upon the consciousness of every man who is more than a patent digester. There is a moral in *Don Quixote*, and a very profound one, whether Cervantes consciously put it there or not, and it is this: that whoever quarrels with the Nature of Things, wittingly or unwittingly, is certain to get the worst of it. The great difficulty lies in finding out what the Nature of things really and perdura-

bly is, and the great wisdom, after we have made this discovery, or persuaded ourselves that we have made it, is in
accommodating our lives and actions to it as best we may
or can. And yet, though all this be true, there is another
and deeper moral in the book than this. The pathos which
underlies its seemingly farcical turmoil, the tears which
sometimes tremble under our lids after its most poignant
touches of humor, the sympathy with its hero which
survives all his most ludicrous defeats and humiliations
and is only deepened by them, the feeling that he is after
all the one noble and heroic figure in a world incapable
of comprehending him, and to whose inhabitants he is
distorted and caricatured by the crooked panes in those
windows of custom and convention through which they
see him,—all this seems to hint that only he who has
the imagination to conceive and the courage to attempt
a trial of strength with what foists itself on our senses as
the Order of Nature for the time being can achieve great
results, or kindle the cooperative and efficient enthusiasm of his fellow-men. The Don Quixote of one generation may live to hear himself called the savior of society
by the next.

Lowell's argument that someone perceived as a lunatic in
his own time can gradually ignite the participation of others,
and therefore be perceived as a visionary to future generations,
seems particularly relevant to the American condition, after the
Civil War, as leaders strove to fix—sometimes quixotically—
what seemed to be a broken country.

▼ ▼ ▼

IN TWENTIETH-CENTURY AMERICA, Don Quixote became a man for all seasons, a cornucopia of possibilities. For some he was a revolutionary figure, for others the emblem of social justice. John Dos Passos wrote a 1922 travel book on Spain called *Rosinante* [sic] *to the Road Again*, in which he uses the knight-errant's horse as an excuse to wander—and wonder— what the laid-back Spanish people are like (in comparison with work-driven Americans) in the aftermath of the First World War. At one point, one of Dos Passos's friends tells him that in Spain "we live from the belly and loins, or else from the head and heart: between Don Quixote the mystic and Sancho Panza the sensualist there is no middle ground." Later on, Dos Passos turns that vision into a philosophy of Spain, one oscillating between two poles, the warp and the woof:

> And predominant in the Iberian mind is the thought *La vida es sueño*: "Life is a dream." Only the individual, or that part of life which is in the firm grasp of the individual, is real. The supreme expression of this lies in the two great figures that typify Spain for all time: Don Quixote and Sancho Panza; Don Quixote, the individualist who believed in the power of man's soul over all things, whose desire included the whole world in himself; Sancho, the individualist to whom all the world was food for his belly. On the one hand we have the ecstatic figures for whom the power of the individual soul has no limits, in whose minds the universe is but

one man standing before his reflection, God. These are the Loyolas, the Philip Seconds, the fervid ascetics like Juan de la Cruz, the originals of the glowing tortured faces in the portraits of El Greco. On the other hand are the jovial materialists like the Archpriest of Hita, culminating in the frantic, mystical sensuality of such an epic figure as Don Juan Tenorio. Through all Spanish history and art the threads of these two complementary characters can be traced, changing, combining, branching out, but ever in substance the same. Of this warp and woof have all the strange patterns of Spanish life been woven.

As for John Steinbeck, he "discovered" *El Quijote* late in life. In a letter he wrote at the age of fifty to Pascal Covici, his Romanian Jewish American editor at Viking Press in New York, about writing a prologue to his new novel *East of Eden* (1952), Steinbeck states:

> Miguel Cervantes invented the modern novel and with his *Don Quixote* set a mark high and bright. In his prologue, he said best what writers feel—the gladness and the terror.
>
> "Idling reader," Cervantes wrote, "you may believe me when I tell you that I should have liked this book, which is the child of my brain, to be the fairest, the sprightliest and the cleverest that could be imagined, but I have not been able to contravene the law of nature which would have it that like begets like—"

> And so it is with me, Pat. Although some times I have felt that I held fire in my hands and spread a page with shining—I have never lost the weight of clumsiness, of ignorance, of aching inability.

Steinbeck also began a novel titled *Don Keehan*, resetting Cervantes's classic in the American West, but he left it unfinished. As it happens, Roy Williams, an eccentric Texas millionaire obsessed with *El Quijote*, purchased the unpublished manuscript in 2010. Williams was unwilling to allow it to be published because he himself was planning on finishing Cervantes's novel. As I show in the next chapter, this wasn't the first or the last time an editor, translator, or entrepreneur took ownership of *El Quijote*.

Like Sainte-Beuve, William Faulkner believed *El Quijote* to be the source of all literary sources. In the *Paris Review* interview published in the spring of 1956, he said, "Cervantes, *Don Quixote*—I read that every year, as some do the Bible." As several critics have noted, the comic aspects of his fictional Yoknapatawpha County, the setting for a large portion of his oeuvre, spring from Cervantes's fictionalized La Mancha. Closer to the fin de siècle, another American fan, Susan Sontag, in a 1985 essay called "*España: Todo bajo el sol*," originally published as part of a National Tourist Board of Spain catalogue, talked about Cervantes's novel as a narrative of habit, dependence, and obsession:

> The first and greatest epic about addiction, *Don Quixote* is both a denunciation of the establishment of literature and a rhapsodic call to literature. *Don Quixote*

is an inexhaustible book, whose subject is everything (the whole world) and nothing (the inside of someone's head—that is, madness). Relentless, verbose, self-cannibalizing, reflexive, playful, irresponsible, accretive, self-replicating—Cervantes' book is the very image of that glorious *mise-en-abîme* which is literature, and of that fragile delirium which is authorship, its manic expansiveness.

A writer is first of all a reader—a reader gone berserk; a rogue reader; an impertinent reader who claims to be able to do it *better*. Yet, justly, when the greatest living author composed his definitive fable about the writer's vocation, he invented an early-twentieth-century writer who had chosen as his most ambitious work to write (parts of) *Don Quixote*. Once again. Exactly as is (was). For *Don Quixote*, more than any book ever written, *is* literature.

Likewise, John Barth, Thomas Pynchon, Don DeLillo, and David Foster Wallace include references to it in their work. And novelist Kathy Acker wrote a punk, maddening female version in 1986, a rewriting called *Don Quixote: Which Was a Dream*, in which the knight is presented as a woman who, after an abortion scene at the beginning, embarks, along with her sidekick cowboy, Saint Simeon, on a journey where good becomes evil, searching for love "in a world in which love isn't possible." American critic William P. Childers, author of *Transnational Cervantes* (2006), has explored these and other literary resonances. He sees *El Quijote* as the *ur*-text of a generous portion of twentieth-century American fiction, from F. Scott Fitzgerald to Saul Bellow:

James Gatz's reading of rags-to-riches dime novels leads him to transform himself into the enamored Jay Gatsby. His parties function like a knight's heroic deeds; through them he hopes to win back Daisy, his Dulcinea. In *The Dharma Bums*, Kerouac's Japhy Ryder is a counter-culture Quixote who dreams of a "rucksack revolution" that will replace postwar consumerism with an oppositional self fusing New England Transcendentalism and Zen Buddhism. Saul Bellow's Moses Herzog, a Jewish-American existentialist on a quest for authentic selfhood, insists that he is no Quixote, for this is the "post-quixotic U.S.A." But Bellow seems to view this declaration ironically. Whether getting beyond Quixotism is desirable or not, it may not be *possible*.

And in contemporary art, Barry Moser, known for *The Pennyroyal Caxton Bible* (1999), made a famous engraving of Don Quixote riding Rocinante, holding his spear in his right hand. He is proud yet lonesome.

Of course, the embrace of the quixotic in American life wasn't only literary. William Randolph Hearst, the newspaper magnate and the inspiration for Orson Welles's *Citizen Kane* (1941), enjoyed portraying himself as quixotic. So did Cesar E. Chavez, the labor organizer. Obituaries of the Reverend Martin Luther King Jr. describe him as such, as do depictions—including self-descriptions—of Jack Kevorkian, who died in 2011 and was known as "Doctor Death" for encouraging the acceptance of euthanasia among terminally ill patients. Barack Obama, in turn, has been repeatedly criticized by his opponents—and, tellingly, by his supporters as well—as quixotic

Quixote and Rocinante (2004), *by Barry Moser.*

in his idealism, in his incapacity to look at windmills for what they are. What distinguishes them all is their commitment to a dream and their belief in their own exceptional qualities.

Given all this, it is astounding that no Hollywood movie has ever been completed. Indeed, the history of film adaptations of Cervantes's novel is rich in misbegotten ventures, among the most notorious of which is a multi-nation project lead by Orson Welles. In 1956, when he came up with the idea for an adaptation while on *The Frank Sinatra Show*, Welles had a penchant for complex projects and, because of his reputation as a difficult auteur, often encountered trouble as he sought to raise money in the United States.

Charlton Heston, famous for his Bible movie *The Ten Commandments*, released that same year, was scheduled early on to play the leading role. But other commitments interfered, and Heston never quite got on board. Undeterred, Welles began filming in 1957, with Francisco Reiguera as the knight-errant and Akim Tamiroff as his squire. The black-and-white cinematography, as is frequently the case in his films, is wonderful.

Short of funds, Welles had the editing done (poorly) in Spain, where the voice-over was produced in Spanish. Then, having moved on to other projects, and after being pushed out by his own Hollywood studio from the editing of *Touch of Evil* (1958), Welles went to Mexico. There, using his own money, he filmed some more scenes for his Quixote narrative. Patty McCormack, who had just been part of the cast of *El Cid* (1961), was scheduled to play Dulcinea.

In 1964, Welles said the movie was almost done, yet no release was scheduled. Then, in the 1970s, Reiguera and Tamiroff died. A forty-four-minute clip was shown at the Cannes Film Festival. There are scenes of a cemetery, bullfighting, a movie theater. Apparently, the film was meant to begin with Welles reading the story of Don Quixote to a girl. Once the storytelling ends, Sancho Panza appears in person. At one point, Welles plays a director, looking to cast Sancho in a movie by Orson Welles.

Still, there is a version remixed by Jesús Franco (the Spanish director of the singularly awful B-movie, among others from him, titled *The Awful Dr. Orloff* [known in Spanish as *Gritos en la noche*, 1961]) and produced by the Spaniard Patxi Irigoyen. It is a dissatisfying hodgepodge with recognizably little connection to Welles's original intentions. Aside from the fact that countless legal hurdles prevented them from getting all the available footage, Franco and Irigoyen were not the right match for Welles, who in any case was always weary of others re-editing his work. The movie premiered at the Cannes Film Festival in 1992 to a whimper of a response and was generally considered a flop. The scene of the windmills, however, is intriguing. As the knight-errant comes upon them, one windmill grows in size, and as Don Quixote begins his battle, macabre sounds play in the background while the scenes with Don Quixote are juxtaposed with stills from paintings by Goya. There's also an exciting section in which the odd couple enters a movie theater. Sancho tries a lollipop Dulcinea gives him. The two watch the screen, but it is Don Quixote who is enthralled by the projections he sees. At some point, he jumps on stage and attempts to battle the images on the screen. Welles obviously was seeking an innovative, experimental approach, which might have been what caused the demise of his ill-fated enterprise. We shall never fully know what he envisioned for his adaptation of *Don Quixote*; it was still incomplete when he died in 1985.

Ironically, however, in the end he did complete *Nella terra di Don Chisciotte* (In the Land of Don Quixote), a nine-episode Italian documentary on Spain. It was shot in 1961, but it didn't air until 1964. The entire series isn't directly linked to Cervantes's novel, but its atmosphere is inspired by it.

▼ ▼ ▼

TERRY GILLIAM, THE AMERICAN-BORN British member of the Monty Python troupe, tried to make a free adaptation of *El Quijote* in 1998. It was supposed to feature a twenty-first-century marketing executive who is thrown back to the seventeenth century. The cast included Jean Rochefort as Don Quixote and Johnny Depp as Sancho Panza. Yet despite a budget of $32.1 million, the effort collapsed after a series of mishaps, including insurance issues, the destruction of equipment during a flood, and Rochefort's illness. In 2002, directors Keith Fulton and Louis Pepe made a fascinating documentary called *Lost in La Mancha*, about Gilliam's cinematic misadventure, in which they explored the calamities that befell the production. Over the years, Rochefort was replaced, first by Robert Duvall, then by Ewan McGregor, and a new attempt to make the film took place in 2008. Again, the movie failed to materialize. In 2014, word came out that Gilliam had secured new financing and that, with a new screenplay, the film would finally be concluded.

Fittingly, one of the most popular twentieth-century American artifacts connected with *El Quijote* is the schmaltzy song "The Impossible Dream," known as "The Quest." Composed by Mitch Leigh, with lyrics by Joe Darion, the song is the centerpiece of Dale Wasserman's Broadway musical *Man of La Mancha*, which premiered in 1965.

The show started as a CBS telecast play, not a musical, written by Wasserman, with Lee J. Cobb, Colleen Dewhurst, and Eli Wallach. It was broadcast on November 9, 1959, to an estimated audience of twenty million viewers, as part of a series sponsored by the DuPont chemical company. DuPont, however, didn't

Poster for the 2002 documentary by Keith Fulton and Louis Pepe, on the filmic quest by Terry Gilliam to adapt Don Quixote.

like the name *Man of La Mancha* because it thought Americans wouldn't know what La Mancha was, so the title was changed to *I, Don Quixote*. The script was then unsuccessfully optioned for a Broadway play. Producer Albert Marre (née Albert Eliot Moshinsky) finally suggested Wasserman turn it into a musical.

The team originally commissioned poet W. H. Auden, a veteran of opera lyrics (among others, he wrote the libretto of Benjamin Britten's *Paul Bunyan* [1941]), to write the lyrics with his longtime friend and sometime lover Chester Kallman. But Auden and Wasserman didn't see eye to eye. Wasserman wanted an idealistic Don Quixote, whereas Auden, in Wasserman's account in *The Impossible Musical: The "Man of La Mancha" Story* (2003), believed the knight-errant "must repudiate his quest and warn others against like folly." A version of Auden's lyrics survives, such as this decidedly brazen portion about Dulcinea:

> Look! Those noble knights of old
> Were, when the whole truth is told,
>   All crooks.
> Look at Dulcinea! Mutt!
> She's the common kitchen slut
>   She looks.

Rex Harrison was supposed to play the knight-errant, who is also Cervantes in the production. But he was busy, and the role went to Richard Kiley, who won a Tony Award in 1966 for his performance and was the first to sing "The Impossible Dream." Every decade or so there is another Broadway revival. The movie adaptation of the musical, with Peter O'Toole, Sophia Loren, and Ian Richardson, and directed by Canadian film-maker Arthur Hiller, was released in 1972.

The majority of people exposed to *Man of La Mancha* actually come to the novel through the film. And the song "The Impossible Dream" sticks like chewing gum. There is something innately American in this mantra: the self is at the core of all adventures, and each of us needs to protect our own self, make it flourish. Adversity prevails in the world. Still, to fight for one's own dreams is to know their true worth.

Scores of musicians—from Elvis to Liberace, from Tom Jones and Julio Iglesias to Donna Summer—have performed

Poster for the 1965 musical, which, along with its Hollywood
adaptation with Peter O'Toole, is arguably the entry door for many
to Cervantes's Don Quixote.

"The Impossible Dream." The most popular version is sung by
Frank Sinatra, who, with a debonair delivery, makes you feel
you should never renounce your own goals.

There is also someone who is famous for *not* singing the
song—John Cleese. The Monty Python comedian was supposed
to sing it in 1977 on *The Muppet Show*. Kermit the Frog introduces Cleese with fanfare, telling the audience that the actor
will be singing "The Impossible Dream." Cleese misses his cue,
however, and says to Kermit, "I don't do old show tunes." Kermit tries again, and the next time the curtain goes up, Cleese is

dressed as a warrior and standing beside a human-sized monster puppet. Cleese protests again, and the final time the curtain rises, Cleese is dressed as a maraca musician. Still, no song comes out. As he prepares to leave the stage, scores of Muppets surround him, repeating everything he says in song until they finally belt out some lines to "The Impossible Dream."

In the infinite sequence of *El Quijote*'s reverberations through time, Cleese's reluctance to perform the Broadway song might be a litmus test. One of the world's most popular novels, itself an artifact of popular culture in Renaissance Spain, which, through the centuries, had become the property of a highbrow, sophisticated elite, had now returned to its roots. And, fittingly, in that very return it was, once again, the subject of ridicule.

THE UNITED STATES IN the twenty-first century is as quixotic as ever. For one thing, exceptionalism is ingrained in the nation's spirit, both at home and in foreign policy. In spite of the gridlock in Washington, the country's sense of its own uniqueness remains unchanged. Meanwhile, the Latino population of almost 60 million (out of a total of 320 million Americans) is already the largest minority and in some places a majority. Even though *El Quijote* was written in Spain, about which Hispanics have ambivalent feelings, they see it as their—our—own masterpiece, the one classic that has unquestionably shaped our culture.

Latinos were in the United States even before the nation became a nation in 1776, and they have been propagating a

First page of a cartoon adaptation of Don Quixote *into Spanglish,*
by David Enriquez and Ilan Stavans.

rich, diverse literary tradition that extends from Alvar Núñez
Cabeza de Vaca's *Chronicle of the Narváez Expedition*, about the
1527 shipwreck he was involved in and his subsequent trek
through Florida and other parts of the future country, to contemporary works by authors such as Oscar Hijuelos, Gloria
Anzaldúa, and Junot Díaz. It should go without saying that

Cervantes's masterpiece is often a source of inspiration, as it surely was for María Amparo Ruiz de Burton, considered the first Hispanic author in the United States to write a novel in English. Her novel *The Squatter and the Don* (1885) is about land-ownership disputes in California after the Guadalupe Hidalgo Treaty of 1848. Less than a decade before her novel appeared, she adapted *El Quijote* for the stage. Her version is called *Don Quixote de la Mancha: A Comedy in Five Acts, Taken from Cervantes' Novel of That Name*. It was published and performed in San Francisco in 1876. Although it follows *El Quijote* quite closely, Ruiz de Burton stressed the comedic in her adaptation and, more importantly, introduced a strong political message, portraying the knight-errant and his squire as fighters against larger corporate abuse, a topic that appears in her fiction as well.

Another crucial Chicano work influenced by *El Quijote* is Daniel Venegas's episodic novel *The Adventures of Don Chipote; or, A Sucker's Tale* (1928), which explores the life of poor immigrants in the United States after the Mexican Revolution of 1910. But the impact has also been strong among other Latinos, especially Puerto Ricans. Jesús Colón makes various references to Cervantes in his collection of vignettes, *A Puerto Rican in New York, and Other Sketches* (1961), about the arrival of Puerto Rican *jíbaros*, rural workers from the island, in New York City. A union organizer who was called to testify in front of the House Un-American Activities Committee in Washington, D.C., during the McCarthy era, Colón was a precursor to the Nuyorican Movement, an artistic explosion of activists, poets, novelists, and musicians in the 1960s and 1970s. His variety of *Quijotismo* looks at Puerto Ricans as a people marked by a powerful culture that is defined by idealism, whose desire to assimilate into the United States often pushes them to choose between materialism and remaining loyal to their dreams.

This is right: Cervantes's novel is the banner, the pledge of allegiance, the constitution of Hispanic civilization, including the portion—the nation within the nation—living north of the Rio Grande.

10

FLEMISH TAPESTRIES

endered into some fifty languages (there are approximately five thousand languages in the world today), *El Quijote* is one of the most translated novels in history. Its length probably hinders it from translation to some extent, or it would surely surpass classics such as *Alice in Wonderland* (ninety-seven languages), *Adventures of Huckleberry Finn* (sixty-five), Chinua Achebe's *Things Fall Apart* (fifty), and popular fiction like Paolo Coelho's *The Alchemist* and J. K. Rowling's *Harry Potter* saga (both sixty-seven). (Unsurprisingly, in terms of the number of translations into which a book has been rendered, the Bible is the undisputed winner.)

Spanish, of course, was Cervantes's mother tongue. But, as previously mentioned, he lived temporarily in Naples, Italy, where he was stationed in the *Infantería de Marina*. And, on his way back to Spain, he was captured with his brother in the Mediterranean Sea and held captive in Algiers. He might at least have been acquainted with Italian and Arabic and was maybe even fluent in those languages. As a member of the intellectual elite of his time, he also knew some basic Latin. Unquestionably, Cervantes's existential sojourns and his lifelong learning sensitized him to the nuances of language.

This, and the folklore around Cide Hamete Benengeli's lost palimpsest (a theme I explored in chapter 4, "A Modern Novel"), explains why *El Quijote* is built as a celebration not only of the act of reading but also of translation. The novel mentions authors like Cicero, Horace, and Torquato Tasso, as well as the works of Aristotle and *La Chanson de Roland* (circa 1040). And, of course, Don Quixote's entire journey is based on his compulsive reading of chivalry novels by Amadis of Gaul and Tirant lo Blanc, among others, all of which were translated into Spanish from French, Italian, Portuguese, and Catalan, not to mention Latin.

In addition to the commentary surrounding the translator of Benengeli's work, translation becomes a topic of discussion in the novel's Second Part, chapter LXII, as Don Quixote and Sancho reach Barcelona. Their wanderings finally take them to the print shop, the equivalent of a modern bookstore where authors and translators gather, as well as a place equipped with machines to print books. The two end up speaking there with a translator (from the Italian into the Spanish):

> "I would venture to swear," said Don Quixote, "that your worship is not known in the world, which always begrudges their reward to rare wits and praiseworthy labours. What talents lie wasted there! What genius thrust away into cor-

ners! What worth left neglected! Still it seems to me that translation from one language into another, if it be not from the queens of languages, the Greek and the Latin, is like looking at Flemish tapestries on the wrong side; for though the figures are visible, they are full of threads that make them indistinct, and they do not show with the smoothness and brightness of the right side; and translation from easy languages argues neither ingenuity nor command of words, any more than transcribing or copying out one document from another. But I do not mean by this to draw the inference that no credit is to be allowed for the work of translating, for a man may employ himself in ways worse and less profitable to himself. This estimate does not include two famous translators, Doctor Cristobal de Figueroa, in his Pastor Fido, and Don Juan de Jauregui, in his Aminta, wherein by their felicity they leave it in doubt which is the translation and which the original. But tell me, are you printing this book at your own risk, or have you sold the copyright to some bookseller?"

"Like looking at Flemish tapestries on the wrong side." In Don Quixote's view, translation diminishes rather than expounds meaning; instead of bringing light and clarity to a text, it darkens, it obfuscates. This is a rather pessimistic view for a book like *El Quijote*, which purports to be a translation—and a rather impromptu one, made by a *morisco aljamiado*—from the Arabic and which, ironically, has been accessed by the vast majority of its own readers in a language other than its original Spanish. Could it be that countless readers have only appreciated it from the wrong side?

▼ ▼ ▼

THE TRANSLATORS OF *El Quijote* have been a rather motley gang. Officially, English isn't the first language into which Cervantes's novel was translated. César Oudin rendered the novella *The Ill-Conceived Curiosity*, featured in the First Part of *El Quijote*, into French in 1608, three years after it appeared in the original. Six years later, Oudin himself would translate the entire First Part. He followed it with a translation of the Second Part—thus completing a translation of the entire novel— in 1618.

France is notorious for having produced one of the most fraudulent of all translations, a truncated rendition by François Filleau de Saint-Martin. It was published in four volumes in 1677 under the title *Histoire de l'admirable Don Quichotte de*

Title page of the 1678 French translation by Francois Filleau de Saint-Martin, which added an apocryphal final chapter.

la Manche. Filleau de Saint-Martin deliberately sent the book to the printer without the last chapter because—*mirabile dictum*—he himself dreamed of writing a third part, composed of completely new adventures of the knight-errant and his squire, and maybe even a fourth.

Indeed, once his work as a translator was finished, Filleau de Saint-Martin wrote—in French—a version in which Don Quixote regains his use of reason and anoints his squire Sancho Panza a knight. Then, the couple sets out to continue their quest to mend the world. The sequence of events becomes muddy, not only in terms of the action but also because of the choice of narrative voice. One of their rendezvous is retold by a French dame and includes among its protagonists two more women, Silvia and Sainville.

Italians have a saying, *tradutore, tradittore,* meaning all translators are traitors. Rather than perceiving his task as simply bringing a text from the original to the target language, the French translator understood it more creatively, to the point of competing with Cervantes, or at least completing what in his view Cervantes had left unfinished. In any case, ironically, the French translator died before coming to the end of the sequel, which was then finished by Robert Challe, his pupil and a renowned literary figure at the end of the seventeenth and beginning of the eighteenth century. At the end of the story, Don Quixote dies after drinking water from a well he believed to be the Fountain of Forgetting.

At any rate, there are more translations of *El Quijote* into English than into any other language. In fact, other than the Bible, no book has been translated into Shakespeare's tongue as often. Here is the list of English translators, with the date of publication of their work in parenthesis:

Thomas Shelton (1612)
John Phillips (1687)
Peter Anthony Motteux (1700–1703)
John Stevens (1700)
Charles Jervas (1742)
Tobias Smollett (1755)
George Kelley (1769)
T. T. Shore (1864)
Alexander J. Duffield (1881)
John Ormsby (1885)
Henry Edward Watts (1888)
Robinson Smith (1910)
Samuel Putnam (1949)
J. M. Cohen (1950)
Walter Starkie (1954)
Burton Raffel (1995)
John Rutherford (2000)
Edith Grossman (2003)
Tom Lathrop (2005)
James H. Montgomery (2009)

In the face of such plentitude, the question arises: what language is richer in quixotic endeavors, Spanish or English? Spanish obviously owns the one and only sacred text. And its very sacredness deems it inalterable. For *Cervantistas*, changing even a dot or a conjugation in *El Quijote* is anathema. Attempts at modernizing it are often met with controversy. In English, on the other hand, the permutations are infinite. Each translator gives free range to his or her talent, creating a narrative that is also defined by the way the language is used in that particular historical moment.

I once set myself the task, during one full year, of reading all English translations available to that point. It was a fascinating (if also exhausting) undertaking. In doing so, one witnesses the changes of the English language through time, from its Elizabethan variety in the early seventeenth century to the one we use today, four hundred years later. The linguistic transformation becomes obvious against this historical procession: spelling and conjugations have changed; verb choices are different; and while articles and pronouns appear to be the most stable, they too have undergone a change in function.

Four of the English translators are American; the rest are British. One was a mailman; another was a painter. Several were professors. A number of them, including J. M. Cohen and Burton Raffel, were specialists in European languages, rendering into English works by Horace, Columbus, Montaigne, Teresa de Ávila, Rabelais, and Pasternak, as well as the *Nibelungenlied*. Walter Starkie, an Irish Hispanist who taught at the University of California, Los Angeles, knew Romany, the language of the gypsies, and was an authority on them. He was a worldwide traveler (*Time* magazine, in a profile, described him as a modern-day gypsy). His godfather was John Pentland Mahaffy, Oscar Wilde's tutor.

More than one rendition reads as a hodgepodge of earlier translations into English, although only one translator gets the credit. And, in what seems like a hoax worthy of a Hollywood blockbuster movie, it is often repeated that one of the translators didn't speak a single word of Spanish. But I should start at the beginning. About Thomas Shelton, the first on the list—the trendsetter—little is known. It appears that he was a personal letter carrier in London. He also served as a mailman in Dublin for the improbably named Sir William FitzWilliam, an English official in Ireland in the late sixteenth century. Later on, he was employed by Thomas Howard, who was the Earl of Walden, later Earl of Suffolk. Nothing remains of his work as a translator except his rendition of *El Quijote*, entitled *The Historie of the Valorous and Wittie Knight-Errant Don-Quixote of the Mancha*. Shelton completed the translation of the First Part in 1607 but didn't publish it—perhaps because he struggled to find a printer to bring it out—until 1612. He didn't use the Spanish original, published by Juan de la Cuesta, as his source. Instead, Shelton had in front of him the pirated edition of the Spanish one made in Brussels in 1607. For the Second Part, he did use the legitimate Madrid edition. His translation appeared in 1620.

In the dedication to the First Part—to his patron, the Earl of Suffolk—he states that he "translated some five or six yeares agoe, *The Historie of Don-Quixote*, out of the Spanish tongue, into the English . . . in the space of forty daies: being therunto more than half enforced, through the importunitie of a very deere friend, that was desirous to understand the subject." It is known that Shelton approached the king of Spain on his patron's behalf and that the patron's wife, Catherine, Lady Suffolk, received an annual payment of one thousand pounds a year from the Spanish royals, although it is unclear why. Suspicions abound that Shelton and Lady Suffolk were involved in espionage. There is speculation as well that on his trips to Madrid, Shelton met Cervantes, but none of these hypotheses have been proved true.

Needless to say, forty days seems like a record—even impossible—time frame for such an ambitious endeavor, considering that the original (the First Part only) has a length of roughly 180,000 words. There is debate over whether Shelton was indeed the translator of the First Part, since stylistically the translations of the two parts are different. Among those questioning the second effort are Alexander J. Duffield, who himself translated the novel in 1881. (His own rendition is largely forgotten.)

Since Shelton's version uses Tudor English, it is seldom read now, although it remains in print. It was quite popular for at least 150 years, serving as the model against which to compete. James Fitzmaurice-Kelly, an early-twentieth-century British scholar of Spanish literature, Cervantes biographer, and fellow of the British Academy, as well as a member of the *Real Academia Española*, prepared an edition of the Shelton version in 1890. He considered Shelton to be "Lord of the golden Elizabethan speech." Fitzmaurice-Kelly stated, he "manifests himself an exquisite in the noble style, an expert in the familiar and with such effect as no man has matched in England."

Successive translators have been less generous with Shelton. This is understandable: to pitch the making of a new translation, not only to a potential publisher but also to a readership interested in fresh new versions, many translators begin by discrediting previous translations. Since Shelton is the first in line, he receives the toughest blows. Take Charles Jervas, a popular Irish portrait painter (his portraits of Jonathan Swift and

Alexander Pope hang in London's National Portrait Gallery), whose translation of *El Quijote* was published posthumously in 1742, three years after his death. His translation misspelled his name on the title page as "Jarvis," a typo that stuck forever. As it happens, the "Jarvis version" was the most popular in eighteenth-century England. In his preface, Jarvis accuses Shelton of translating not from the original but from the Italian rendition by Lorenzo Franciosini. Yet Franciosini's translation was not published until 1622, two years after Shelton released his own version of the Second Part.

Undeterred, Jarvis makes the following case:

> In the ninth chapter of the third book of the first part, Sancho's ass is stolen by Gines de Passamonte, while Sancho is asleep; and presently after, the author mounts him again in a very remarkable manner, sideways like a woman, *a la mugeriega*. This story being but imperfectly told, Franciosini took it for a gross oversight: he therefore alters it, indeed a little unhappily; for, in defect of the ass, he is forced to put Sancho's wallets and provender upon Rozinante, though the wallets were stopt before by the inn-keeper, in the third chapter of the third book. This blundering amendment of the translator is literally followed by Shelton.
>
> Again, in pursuance of this, Franciosini alters another passage in the eleventh chapter of the same book. Sancho says to his master, who had enjoined him absolute silence: If beasts could speak as they did in the days of Guisopete (I suppose he means Aesop) my case would not be quite so bad; for then I might commune with my ass, and say

what I pleased to him. Here the Italian makes him "Commune with Rozinante"; and Shelton follows him with this addition, "Since my niggardly fortune has deprived me of my ass."

Further along, Jarvis wonders if Cervantes made the mistake in order to make readers (including translators) stumble foolishly:

> But what if Cervantes made this seeming slip on purpose for a bait to tempt his minor criticks; in the same manner as, in another place, he makes the princess of Micomicon land at Ossuna, which is no sea-port? As by that he introduced a fine piece of satire on an eminent Spanish historian of his time, who had described it as such in his history; so by this he might only take occasion to reflect on a parallel incident in Ariosto, where Brunelo, at the siege of Albraca, steals the horse from between the legs of Sacripante king of Circassia. It is the very defense he makes for it, in the fourth chapter of the second part, where, by the way, both the Italian and old English translators have preserved the excuse, though by their altering the text they have taken away the occasion of it.

In truth, it was the Italian translator Franciosini who consulted Shelton. But this wouldn't have deterred Jarvis from discrediting his predecessors.

Taking a somewhat different approach is John Ormsby, a professional British translator who worked in the second half of the nineteenth century. In his long introduction, he discusses at length various early translation efforts. He simultaneously praises and attacks Shelton. On the one hand, he writes, "His fine old crusted English would, no doubt, be relished by a minority, but it would be only by a minority. His warmest admirers must admit that he is not a satisfactory representative of Cervantes. His translation of the First Part was very hastily made and was never revised by him. It has all the freshness and vigor, but a full measure of the faults, of a hasty production. It is often very literal—barbarously literal frequently—but just as often very loose. He had evidently a good colloquial knowledge of Spanish, but apparently not much more. It never seems to occur to him that the same translation of a word will not suit in every case."

On the other hand, Ormsby sees Shelton for what he is: the first. That is, he inaugurated a tradition. He writes that Shelton "had the inestimable advantage of belonging to the same generation as Cervantes; *Don Quixote* had to him a vitality that only a contemporary could feel; it cost him no dramatic effort to see things as Cervantes saw them; there is no anachronism in his language; he put the Spanish of Cervantes into the English of Shakespeare." The last statement is remarkable. It grants us an opportunity to meditate on various approaches to a classic. For Shelton, *El Quijote* was a popular contemporary book. Yet for Ormsby, as well as for anyone sufficiently distanced from the original publications in 1605 and 1615, it is a historical artifact. A translator of a contemporary work moves from one linguistic present to another. Ormsby, on the other hand, needed to travel from the past (early-seventeenth-century Spanish) to his present (late-nineteenth-century English). He needed to make his own reader feel Cervantes's time without re-creating Shakespeare's language. All this invites these questions: Could someone today produce a *historical* translation into English of *El Quijote*? Would it read like Shelton's version, which Ormsby calls "a racy old version," one that "with all its defects, has a charm that no modern translation, however skillful or correct, could possess?"

SHELTON, IN ANY CASE, is not the only guinea pig. Another member of the gang, Peter Anthony Motteux, also called Pierre Antoine Motteux, famous for delivering *El Quijote* with a Cockney accent, is also a favorite target. His translation, released in four volumes starting in 1700, is probably the most frequently reprinted, often in revised form. This is bizarre, given how untrustworthy it is. Worse even, it does not appear to have been really his.

Again, biographical information on Motteux is scarce. A playwright, editor (he was in charge of *The Gentleman's Journal* between 1692 and 1694), and translator, he completed Thomas Urquhart's translation of *Gargantua and Pantagruel*. Motteux was born in Normandy. That is, French was his first tongue. He arrived in England in 1685, at the age of twenty-two. Fifteen years later, he published *The History of the Ingenious Gentleman, Don Quixote of La Mancha*. Can a person only a decade and a half into a life in a new language convey the nuances of a foreign literary text in his adopted tongue?

Motteux seems to have consulted the Spanish editions. He also had at his side the English versions by Shelton and John

Phillips, the latter a nephew of John Milton and another translator of scores of French books as well as *El Quijote*. In addition, Motteux used several versions of *El Quijote* in French and Italian. The use of these variants enabled him to contrast different approaches. Given all this information, the statement on the cover of Motteux's rendition is mind-blowing: "translated from the original by several hands." It provokes numerous questions: Did he hire others to do the job? How was his army of translators composed? Did they know each other? Did they collaborate? What kind of editing was done to homogenize the material? By whom? Or was he simply giving credit to the many sources he had consulted? History doesn't offer an answer to these questions.

Samuel Putnam, an American translator, called Phillip's rendition "the worst ever made," one that "cannot even be called a translation." Ormsby agreed:

> Anyone who compares it carefully with the original will have little doubt that it is a concoction from Shelton and the French of Filleau de Saint Martin, eked out by borrowings from Phillips, whose mode of treatment it adopts. It is, to be sure, more decent and decorous, but it treats "Don Quixote" in the same fashion as a comic book that cannot be made too comic.

What is unquestionable is that the work feels discombobulated. Using sly irony, it often makes fun of the knight-errant and his squire. It is condescending, not to say demeaning. His portraiture of women verges on the obscene. And the translation displays some Cockney jargon. This is the beginning of the

First Part, chapter XVI, which takes place as the knight-errant, beaten up, arrives with his squire at the inn. Motteux's women come to the fore:

> The innkeeper, seeing Don Quixote lying quite athwart the ass, asked Sancho what ailed him. Sancho answered, it was nothing, only his master had got a fall from the top of a rock to the bottom, and he bruised his sides a little. The innkeeper had a wife very different from the common sort of hostesses, for she was a charitable nature, and very compassionate of her neighbor's affliction: which made her immediately take care of Don Quixote, and call her daughter (a good handsome girl) to set her helping hand to his cure. One of the servants in the inn was an Asturian wrench, a broadfaced, flat-handed, saddle-nosed dowry, blind of one eye, and the other almost out. However, the activity of her body supplied all other defects. She was not above three feet high from her heels to her head; and her shoulders, which somewhat loaded her, as having too much flesh upon them, made her look downwards oftener than she could have wished. This charming original likewise assisted the mistress and the daughter; and, with the latter, helped to make the Knight's bed, and a sorry one it was; the room where it stood was an old gambling cock-loft, which by manifold signs seemed to have been, in the days of yore, a repository of chopped straw.

Ormsby is right: to improve the humor of *El Quijote* by "an infusion of cockney flippancy and facetiousness, as Motteux's operators did, is not merely an impertinence like larding a sirloin of prize beef, but an absolute falsification of the spirit of the book, and it is a proof of the uncritical way in which 'Don Quixote' is generally read that this worse than worthless translation—worthless as failing to represent, worse than worthless as misrepresenting—should have been favoured as it has been."

Obviously, as the rowdy gang of English translators of Cervantes became more professionalized, their disapproval of previous renditions was exacerbated. The lack of rigor drove some of them nuts.

Despite its flaws, Motteux's translation made *El Quijote* extraordinarily popular in eighteenth-century London. For instance, Samuel Johnson, ever a hero of mine, once stated, "Was there ever yet anything written by mere man that was wished longer by its readers, excepting *Don Quixote*, *Robinson Crusoe*, and *The Pilgrim's Progress*?" And Lord Byron was a devout admirer of *El Quijote* (as well as of Ariosto's *Orlando furioso* [1516]), and either made reference or else borrowed from it profusely. For instance, Byron discussed Cervantes in *Don Juan*, Canto Thirteen, from the middle of stanza VIII to the end of stanza XI:

> I should be very willing to redress
> Men's wrongs, and rather check than punish crimes,
> Had not Cervantes, in that too true tale
> Of Quixote, shown how all such efforts fail.
>
> Of all tales 't is the saddest—and more sad,
> Because it makes us smile: his hero's right,
> And still pursues the right;—to curb the bad

His only object, and 'gainst odds to fight
His guerdon: 't is his virtue makes him mad!
But his adventures form a sorry sight;—
A sorrier still is the great moral taught
By that real Epic unto all who have thought

Redressing injury, revenging wrong,
To aid the damsel and destroy the caitiff;
Opposing singly the united strong,
From foreign yoke to free the helpless native:—
Alas! must noblest views, like an old song,
Be for mere Fancy's sport a theme creative,
A jest, a riddle, Fame through thin and thick sought!
And Socrates himself but Wisdom's Quixote?

Cervantes smiled Spain's chivalry away;
A single laugh demolished the right arm
Of his own country;—seldom since that day
Has Spain had heroes. While Romance could charm,
The World gave ground before her bright array;
And therefore have his volumes done such harm,
That all their glory, as a composition,
Was dearly purchased by his land's perdition.

While Byron saw the book as the end of an era, others among his contemporaries saw in it the beginning of a new one, full of possibility. By mid-century, Charlotte Lennox fashioned a woman's adaptation called *The Female Quixote: or, The Adventures of Arabella* (1752), which to some is a defining text in the history of the British novel. The heroine is an insatiable reader of French romance novels who loses the sense of the world by believing her life must be defined by adventure, at one point even throwing herself into the Thames in order to escape some horsemen she is sure are haunting her. She speaks of fiction as "more true" than reality. Ultimately, she gives up her quixotic dreams when she agrees to marry her cousin.

In what is perhaps the highest tribute, Laurence Sterne, known as the father of experimental fiction, modeled the character of Uncle Toby in *The Life and Opinions of Tristram Shandy, Gentleman* (1759) after Cervantes's knight-errant. As a whole, Sterne's novel is an embrace of the aesthetic affinities of *El Quijote*: a humorous, self-referential narrative that is concerned with poetry and philosophical questions about life in general (John Locke and the Metaphysical poets are constantly being invoked), all while the reader is being reminded, time and again, that fiction is a conceit, an artifice—not an escape from reality but an anchor in it.

The connection between Cervantes and Sterne, who read *El Quijote* in Motteux's rendition, has been eloquently explored by Milan Kundera. In his essay "The Depreciated Legacy of Cervantes" (part of *The Art of the Novel* [1986]), he writes that Sterne is playful, just like Cervantes, in that he poses lasting philosophical questions while recognizing that philosophy no longer has the answer and that literature—the novel as a literary genre, in particular—is an artifact where ambiguity and the lack of certainty are offered as more suitable answers to the sensibility of modern readers. That, in his view, is how Sterne assimilates Cervantes's legacy—that is, he recognizes that the world doesn't have "a single absolute truth but a welter of contradictory truths (truths embodied in *imaginary selves* called characters)." With the popularity of Motteux's version, and as a result of the desire of other translators to improve on his discombobulated narrative, *El Quijote* was rendered into English a total of four times in the same century. The most controversial of these translations was by Tobias Smollett, the celebrated Scottish author of such novels as *The Adventures of Roderick Random* (1748). Though Carlos Fuentes naively called the Smollett version "the homage of a novelist to a novelist," it has been marred by accusations of impostorship since its release in 1755.

In the translator's note written in the third person, Smollett claims his aim was to maintain that "ludicrous solemnity and self-importance by which the inimitable Cervantes has distinguished the character of Don Quixote, without raising him to the insipid rank of a dry philosopher, or debasing him to the melancholy circumstances and unentertaining caprice of an ordinary madman; and to preserve the native humor of Sancho, from degenerating into mere proverbial phlegm, or affected buffoonery." Smollett adds that the translation "endeavored to retain the spirit and ideas, without servilely adhering to the literal expression, of the original; from which, however, he has not so far deviated, as to destroy the formality of idiom, so peculiar to the Spaniards, and so essential to the character of the work."

That last remark might have been an act of defense *avant la lettre*. In an evasive, unsigned review (by Ralph Griffiths) of Smollett's translation that appeared in *The Monthly Review* in September 1755, the reviewer quietly yet insistently compares the Jarvis and Smollett translations. That he offers no strong opinion on this matter is bizarre since the primary accusation targeted at Smollett is that he copied Jarvis's work without attribution. Perhaps the reviewer was Smollett's friend, or at the very least his acquaintance. There could have been some sense of debt involved. In any case, successive critics have gone further.

The scholar Carmine Rocco Linsalata of Stanford University devoted an entire 1956 study to what he calls "the hoax." In his view, Smollett's translation "is a gem in the realm of fraudulent acts." Analyzing parallel passages from Cervantes, Jarvis, and Smollett, he finds them strikingly similar, if not identical. Second, he compares Smollett to several other previous translators: Shelton, Phillips, Motteux, and Stevens. And, crucially, he spots numerous mistranslations of numbers by Smollett that, damningly, were also mistranslated previously, such as, in the First Part, chapter X, *cuatro o cinco* becoming "three or four," and in chapter VIII, *los primeros días* emerging as "the first two days"; and in the Second Part, chapter II, *docientas* resulting in "a thousand," and in XX, *dos* becoming "a dozen." He uncovers the fact that other arbitrary translations and errors committed by Jarvis were repeated by Smollett, and that Smollett copied Jarvis's footnotes.

Smollett certainly had Jarvis's translation before him. As Rocco Linsalata argued, Smollett plagiarized, paraphrased, rewrote, and inverted Jarvis's translation. This, he believed, was done consistently except in the last three chapters of the First Part. Rocco Linsalata doubted that Smollett even knew Spanish. Since all sorts of strategies are in play, he concluded that the work is not that of a single man but a group. Several Smollett biographers share this view. The members of the novelist's hack school (a practice, by the way, not more common then than it is today) did their job, depending on the biographer, sometime between 1752 and 1763. Why would Smollett engage in such a hoax? With the critical and commercial acclaim following *Roderick Random* in 1748, he was financially stable. Perhaps, since his name would certainly sell books, a hungry publisher approached him to retranslate *El Quijote*.

On a happier note, the club of English translators finally included a woman—and an American to boot—in 2003: Edith Grossman. Prior to rendering *El Quijote* in English, Grossman was known as a professional translator of celebrated Latin American works, including Gabriel García Márquez's *Love in the Time of Cholera*; Álvaro Mutis's *Adventures and Misadventures of Maqroll*; a couple of novels by Mario Vargas Llosa, including *The Feast of the Goat*; and Mayra Montero's books/novels, among them *The Last Night I Spent with You*. But she had also translated novels by Spanish baroque authors like Julián Ríos. And she had worked on Spanish Golden Age poetry, rendering in English the poems of Lope de Vega, Góngora, and Quevedo, among others.

In interviews, Grossman said that she began her effort in February 2001, using Martin de Riquer's edition of 1955, which is based on the first printing of the book and includes discussions of problematic words that emerge from English, French, and Italian translations. This allowed her to have the tradition of *El Quijote* across European languages at her fingertips.

Intriguingly, no recent rendition into English has generated as many accolades as Grossman's. It has been enthusiastically embraced by readers, but it has also been attacked by some *Cervantistas*. Is it because she is female? Or because her inclination is to modernize, to bring the seventeenth-century narrative into the present? One reviewer of her rendition wondered, in an aside, if women read books differently than men. If so, it follows that male and female translators approach a text in divergent fashion. Still, while her approach scandalized the most puritanical of Cervantes scholars who took exception to her overall approach, it pleased a large audience, turning the book into an unexpected best seller. Harold Bloom wrote in his introduction to her translation that "the vitality of [Don Quixote and Sancho's] characterization is more clearly rendered than ever before." Carlos Fuentes called it "a major literary achievement."

Grossman's decisively modern, unadorned style makes the knight-errant's monologues feel crisp and immediate. Her implicit argument for translating in this way was that during Cervantes's own time, his text was neither archaic nor quaint. Instead, he wrote freshly, with an updated verbal reservoir. That is, he was modern before modernity even arrived. So there is no need to make his effort anachronistic, even if, for my taste, "Senor Knight" sounds too streetwise.

COMPARING VARIOUS TRANSLATIONS of *Don Quixote* demonstrates not only the evolution of the English language but also the different choices and liberties our group of translators have taken with the text. I have chosen a segment from the Second Part, chapter XVII, in which Don Quixote faces a cage full of lions, the scene where he utters the famous line "*¿Leoncitos a mí? ¿A mí leoncitos y a tales horas?*" in which the knight-errant displays the type of male bravado I mentioned in the previous section, or a critique of it:

Miguel de Cervantes (1615):

A lo que dijo don Quijote, sonriéndose un poco:

—¿Leoncitos a mí? ¿A mí leoncitos y a tales horas? Pues ¡por Dios que han de ser esos señores que acá los envían si soy yo hombre que se espanta de leones! Apeaos, buen hombre, y pues sois el leonero, abrid esas jaulas y echadme esas bestias fuera, que en mitad desta campaña les daré a conocer quién es don Quijote de la Mancha, a despecho y pesar de los encantadores que a mí los envían.

Thomas Shelton (1620):

To which quoth Don Quixote, smiling a little, "Your lion whelps to me? to me your lion whelps? and at this time of day? Well, I vow to God, your General that sends 'em this way shall know whether I be one that am afraid of lions. Alight, honest fellow, and, if you be the keeper, open their cages, and let me your beasts forth; for I'll make 'em know, in the midst of this champian, who Don Quixote is, in spite of those enchanters that sent 'em."

Peter Anthony Motteux (1700–1703):

What! Said Don *Quixote*, with a scornful Smile, Lion-Whelps against Me! Against Me those puny Beasts! And at this time of Day! Well, I'll make those Gentlemen that sent their Lions this Way, know whether I am a Man to be scar'd with Lions. Get off, honest Fellow; and since you are the Keeper, open their Cages, and let 'em both out; for maugre and in despite of those Inchanters that have sent 'em to try me, I'll make the Creatures know in the midst of this very Field, who *Don Quixote de la Mancha* is.

Charles Jarvis (1742):

At which Don Quixote, smiling a little, said, "To me your lion-whelps! your lion-whelps to me! and at this time of the day! By the living God, those who sent them hither shall see whether I am a man to be scared by lions! Alight, honest friend; and, since you are their keeper, open the cages, and turn out those beasts; for in the midst of this field will I make them know who Don Quixote de la Mancha is, in spite of the enchanters that sent them to me."—

Tobias Smollett (1755):

To which intreaty, Don Quixote answer'd with half a smile, "What are your lion whelps to me, and at this time of day too! Are lion whelps brought against me! I'll make those who sent them hither, yes—by the holy God! I'll make them see whether I am a man to be scared by lions. Come, honest man, get off, and as you are their keeper, open the cages and turn them out; for, in the midst of this plain, will I make the savage beasts of the wilderness know who Don Quixote de la Mancha is, in defiance of the inchanters who have sent them against me."

John Ormsby (1885):

Hereupon, smiling slightly, Don Quixote exclaimed, "Lion-whelps to me! to me whelps of lions, and at such a time! Then, by God! those gentlemen who send them here shall see if I am a man to be frightened by lions. Get down, my good fellow, and as you are the keeper open the cages, and turn me out those beasts, and in the midst of this plain I will let them know who Don Quixote of La Mancha is, in spite and in the teeth of the enchanters who send them to me."

Samuel Putnam (1949):

"Lion whelps against me?" said Don Quixote with a slight smile. "Lion whelps against me? And at such an hour? Then, by god, those gentlemen who sent them shall see whether I am the man to be frightened by lions. Get down, my good fellow, and since you are the lionkeeper, open the cages and turn those beasts out for me; and in the middle of this plain I will teach them who Don Quixote de la Mancha is, notwithstanding and in spite of the enchanters who are responsible for their being here."

J. M. Cohen (1961):

To which Don Quixote replied with a slight smile: "Lion cubs to me? To me lion cubs, and at this time of day? Then I swear to God the gentlemen who have sent them here shall see if I am a man not to be frightened by lions. Get down, my good fellow, and if you are the lion-keeper, open these cages and turn out these beasts for me. For in the middle of this field I will teach them who Don Quixote de la Mancha is, in despite and defiance of the enchanters who have sent them to me."

Burton Raffel (1999):

Don Quijote smiled faintly.

"Lion cubs against me? Against me—lion cubs? And right when they're hungry? Well, we're going to show the gentlemen who sent them here whether I'm the man to worry about a couple of lions! Out of your cart, you, and since you're the lion keeper, open those cages and let these animals come out against me, and right here in the middle of this meadow I'll let them know just who Don Quijote de La Mancha is, and the devil with all the enchanters who sent them here after me."

John Rutherford (2000):

To which Don Quixote said with a smile:

"Lion-whelps now, is it? Is it now lion-whelps, and at this time of day? Well, by God, those fellows sending them here will soon see whether I'm the sort to be afraid of lions! Climb down, my good man and, since you're their innkeeper, open these crates and turn the animals out: here, in the middle of this field, I will show them what sort of a man Don Quixote de la Mancha is, in spite of all the enchanters who have sent them after me."

Edith Grossman (2003):

To which Don Quixote, smiling slightly, said:

"You talk of lions to me? To me you speak of these little lions, and at this hour? Well, by God, those gentlemen who sent them here will see if I am a man who is frightened by lions! Get down, my good man, and since you are the lion keeper, open those cages and bring out those beasts, for in the middle of these fields I shall let them know who Don Quixote de La Mancha is, in spite and in defiance of the enchanters who have sent them to me."

Tom Lathrop (2005):

To which don Quixote said with half a smile: "Little lions for me? For me, little lions, and at this time of day? Well, by God, those men who sent them to me will see if I'm a man to be frightened by lions or not. Get down, my good man, and since you're the lion keeper, open those cages and send those beasts out—for in the middle of this field I'll show them who don Quixote de La Mancha is, in spite of all the enchanters who have sent them to me."

James H. Montgomery (2009):

To which Don Quixote responded with a slight smile:

"Tiny little lions against me? Against me, Don Quixote? And at such hour? Well, by heavens, those gentlemen who have sent them here shall see whether I am a person who fears lions! My good man, since you are the lionkeeper, kindly dismount, open those cages, and release those beasts, for in the middle of this field I shall show them who Don Quixote de La Mancha is despite all the enchanters who may have sent them here."

One sees in these excerpts the gorgeous evolution the English language has undergone over a period of four hundred years. The dashes present at the beginning disappear as versions come closer to our time. Motteux resorts to an archaic and arbitrary use of uppercase letters that became normalized by the mid-twentieth century. Then come the divergent choices. Motteux describes the lions as "Lion-Whelps," whereas Grossman calls them "little lions."

More worrisome—or, depending on how one sees it, perhaps more commendable—are the cases of outright interpretation. Putnam, following Shelton, says, "Lion whelps against me?" the preposition *against* highlighting the threat of the encounter. Rutherford eliminates the emphasis by simply stating, "Lion whelps now, is it?" In this he follows Jarvis, who writes, "To me your lion-whelps!" Smollett modifies Jarvis by announcing, "What are your lion whelps to me, and at this time of day too!"

Whatever opinion one might have about a translator's right—that is, freedom—to interpret, all of these translations are remarkably similar. It can't be otherwise: the task of bringing a text from the source language to the target one allows for some flexibility, but it also has its limits. Translators are working with similar tools applied to the same raw material. Earlier on, I described Smollett as a plagiarist, since in my mind the evidence proves he did not perform the task of translation on his own. But perhaps it is true that all the renditions I have quoted might be described thus.

Less inflammatory and no doubt more pertinent is the question of why all these twenty-plus translations exist, notwithstanding the fact that some are out of print. Once a classic enters the public domain, any publisher is able to capitalize on its enduring bankability. Meanwhile, society changes in its tastes, and language continues to evolve. New renditions are needed because new generations of readers want to access the classic in their own terms, that is, in their own language. And publishers want to continue making profits.

Yet *El Quijote* has not been translated into French this many times, or into any other language for that matter. There is, it seems to me, a unique obsession with the novel in the English-speaking world. This linguistic habitat has constantly made room for it. There is also the fact that English is the lingua franca of today, as Latin was during the Middle Ages and the Renaissance. There are more non-native English-language speakers in the world now than non-native speakers of any other language, making English a global language, nurtured by all sorts of influences and influencing a whole array of cultures. For that reason, the United States and Britain export more translations than do the economically advanced countries in other linguistic habitats, say Germany, France, and even Spain.

Cervantes's is the novel most translated into English because English speakers have identified it as a cornerstone of Western civilization; because they are drawn to it as a source of nourishment for the idealism ingrained in human nature; and because it is an open-ended classic that allows—nay, invites—for multiple interpretations.

▼ ▼ ▼

IN 2002, I WAS PART of a radio show in Barcelona around the topic of Spanglish, the hybrid tongue spoken by millions in the United States and elsewhere. The moderator was talking to me as well as to a member—whose name I do not wish to remember—of the *Real Academia Española*. To understand what transpired on that show, let me offer some context.

For years I have devoted time, energy, and much passion to the analysis of this controversial linguistic phenomenon, thoroughly disliked by purists for its polluted qualities. So let me say it at the outset: Spanglish is beautiful. It is the by-product of two syntactically standardized languages, Spanish and English, which, in constant contact, generate an amorphous crossbreed, a neither-here-nor-there that has grown dramatically since the 1970s as a result of the demographic explosion of the Latino community in the United States.

Spanglish is not solely a verbal manifestation. It is evidence of the arrival of a new *mestizo* culture, for Latinos—that is, people of Hispanic descent living north of the Rio Grande—are already the largest, fastest-growing minority, numbering, according to the 2010 census, more than fifty million and accounting for roughly 15 percent of the country's population.

Just as Cervantes's Spanish was the outcome of an evolution that began with the arrival of the Romans on the Iberian Peninsula, the state of Spanglish might be explained by looking at a number of factors. First, it is not a recent occurrence; the earliest speakers of it—or some proto-manifestation of it— date back to the colonial period, when Spanish explorers and missionaries roamed through what we would come to know as the states of Florida, New Mexico, Arizona, Colorado, Texas, and California, among others. Second, the closeness of Mexico, Cuba, Puerto Rico, the Dominican Republic, and other countries in Latin America to the United States explains its vitality, for Spanglish is not a stepping stone, a middle stage for immigrants and other speakers between the loss of Spanish and the acquisition of English, but, instead, a clearly defined form of communication. And third, just as there is not one Spanish language but numerous varieties (e.g., Argentine, Colombian, Mexican, Panamanian, Venezuelan), rather than a single, unified Spanglish, there are modalities shaped by the origin, age, education, milieu, and date of arrival of Latino immigrants to the United States. These variations, which are often interconnected, include Cubonics, Dominicanish, Nuyorican, Chicano, and others. Likewise, there is an urban Spanglish as well as varieties that pertain to advertising, sports, youth, immigration, and the Internet (i.e., "cyber-Spanglish"), among other possibilities.

In general, Spanglish speakers, in their linguistic exchanges, employ three distinctive strategies: first, code-switching, which means that within the same sentence, they communicate by going back and forth between two standard languages (*I want to rogarte que you should darme el dinero*); second, simultaneous, automatic translation, which happens when a person thinks in one language but communicates in another (*te llamo pa' trás*); and third, the coining of new terms (*el bloque, friqueado, hanguear, la factoría*).

At some point during the radio *chou* in Barcelona, the *RAE* member, recognizing that Spanglish had deep roots, said to me, wisely, that this hybrid tongue ("But is it *really* a language?"

he repeatedly asked) should not be taken seriously unless and until it produces a literary work of the caliber of *El Quijote*. For—in his words, or close to them—"only a language capable of insight is worth our attention."

I told him he was correct. I added that there would surely come a time when such a work would be written, and that, ironically, the work would need to be translated into Spanish or English in order to be understood by speakers of the other language. (Time has proved me right: important works— novels by Julia Alvarez, Oscar Hijuelos, Sandra Cisneros, Cristina García, and Junot Díaz, memoirs by Esmeralda Santiago and Carlos Eire, among others—have been released in translation in the Spanish-speaking world.)

Plus, I said tongue in cheek, it would be delicious to translate *El Quijote* into Spanglish . . . today!

This thought generated much chatter at the end of the show, including a series of call-in comments. As soon as I made it back to my hotel, I found a message left by a newspaper editor asking if I would put my foot where my mouth is and render the First Part, chapter I of *El Quijote* into Spanglish.

I pondered the invitation for a while—honestly, not too long. In retrospect, the fact that such conversation (and the subsequent publication of the translation in the supplement *Cultura/s* of the daily newspaper *La Vanguardia*) took place in the capital of independently minded Catalonia is not, in my view, accidental. After all, this Mediterranean metropolis exists in a state of double consciousness, one in which Spanish and Catalan, as well as Castañol, are spoken.

To add to the list of renditions above, here is the fragment on the *leoncitos* in Spanglish:

To which don Quijote replied, smiling un poco:

"Leoncitos to me? To me leoncitos and at such hours? Pues Dios will show those señores bringing them along if yo soy a man who is frightened by leones! Move aside, good hombre, and if you are the leonero, open those jaulas and let the beasts salir afuera, for in the middle of this campaña I shall let them know who es don Quijote de la Mancha, in spite and in defiance of the encantadores who have sent them a mí."

EPILOGUE

he universe itself contained in its pages? Am I kidding? The Bible of humanity? (Is not the Bible itself "the Bible of humanity"?) These are nothing but exaggerations, hyperboles. *El Quijote* is just another novel, in spite of its echoes.

Still, hyperboles are what literature is about. The central tenet of *El Quijote* is that one must live life in a genuine way, passionately, in spite of what other people think.

Yet passion can cross the line into out-of-control behavior. Cervantes's novel deliberately cautions us against it. Beware of following your own dreams because, although they might set you free, the freedom you get from them is illusory. And beware of a passion for books, since too much reading is dangerous. It blindfolds you. It makes you doubt reality. It makes you believe the world is under a spell. It dries up your brains.

Here is a personal example. Not long ago, while on a trip to

Japan, I stumbled upon a store that could have been the product of a hallucination. It was located near my Tokyo hotel, its name flashing in neon lights simultaneously in Japanese and English: ドンキホーテ and Don Quixote. (The store is often referred to in Japan by the shortened Donki [ドンキ].)

An entire market dedicated to my favorite novel? What other literary character has his own retail business? Would I find action figures of the knight-errant and his squire, their horse and donkey, Dulcinea, bachelor Samson Carrasco, the priest and the barber? Or some of the scores of manga inspired by the novel, illustrating with Japanese-looking characters different segments of Don Quixote's adventures? Or some theme-related lunch boxes, T-shirts, and video games? Would there be a child-friendly area with knights and lions, windmills and castles?

I entered in ecstasy. But at first I found nothing: *nada*. Lots of items, zillions of them: soap bars, baseball uniforms, boxes of cereal, shoelaces, yogurt, hammers, pencils, wallets, Q-tips, air conditioners . . . but nothing connected to the novel.

I asked an employee, but he didn't speak English. He called a manager. He in turn had an English-language vocabulary of less than fifteen words, not enough for me to understand a thing. Ay, how I wished I knew even some rudimentary Japanese. The manager did give me a brochure in English, though. I found out that there are more than 160 Don Quixote branches throughout the country, as well as several more in Hawaii. The brochure offered an array of photos of various items, a list of addresses, and a website. It stated that the first retail store, known as Just Co., opened in the Suginami neighborhood of Tokyo in 1980. A couple of years later, it became a wholesale business.

But why this name? No one knows. I called a number listed in the brochure: no one could tell me. Another customer helped by giving me a loose translation of the word *donki*. Nothing in his explanation related to the actual novel.

Was all this a sign of apathy and disregard toward the source, even an outright affront? I don't know Japanese, but I knew that Japan had a peculiar relationship with the novel. A friend and colleague at Doshisha University in Kyoto had told me that the first partial rendition, by Shujiro Watanabe, was released in 1887 but wasn't based on the original Spanish. It took another sixty years until Hirosada Nagata first translated *El Quijote* from Cervantes's Spanish. That translation was published beginning in 1948, but Nagata never finished it. *A Don Quixote Picture Book* (Ehon Don Kihōte), by stencil-dyer Serizawa Keisuke, a gorgeous example of papermaking craftsmanship done in the tradition of *mingei* folk art, published in Kyoto in 1937, turns the knight into a samurai. While I have never seen the actual book, several collectors have highly praised it to me.

Anyway, the store Donki can obviously not be taken as a sign that Japan has been *quixotized* by the novel, by which I mean it has been enchanted by the story, the way other civilizations have for centuries.

I like the word *quixotized*: it is unlike *quixotic* and *Quijitismo*, suggesting instead a form of acclimation, the effort of becoming adjusted to a certain literary mode, a way of looking at things. To be quixotized is to become sensible to the double consciousness of things, to recognize that yes is not the opposite of no but its complement.

Things are never what they seem. What, then, if I was being deceived? What if Donki was an enchanter's store, the knight-errant nowhere to be found precisely because his entrepreneurial spirit was hidden everywhere in the merchandise? In the First Part, chapter XVII, Don Quixote tells Sancho, "Either

I know little, or this castle is enchanted." Dumbfounded, I wandered around the store, feeling re-energized. Could the tricycle in front of me be the knight-errant's horse Rocinante in disguise? Might that Cabbage Patch doll be Dulcinea? And that huge plastic tray the *yelmo de Mambrino*, a bassinette the knight-errant believes to be his helmet?

Aha!

I felt empowered, exhilarated. I was suddenly convinced I had broken the code.

I tried opening the Q-tips, sure the container held the nails used in the novel to seal a sarcophagus. I would rub these until they revealed their true identity.

"What are you doing? You can't open that, Ilan!" my wife Alison said to me. She had just emerged from a parallel aisle. "We have to pay for it first."

"But . . ."

I was about to explain to her the rationale behind my effort, how I was able to see Donki for what it was. I was in a gallery of concealment, a place at the mercy of Magician Friston. I was inside the world's largest collection of *Quixotalia*, although each of the items had been magically transformed to look like insipid merchandise.

I was sure Alison wouldn't understand. I was sure she would say that I had lost my wits. Still, I felt content with my private truth.

THE TALMUD SAYS THAT every man should accomplish three tasks in life: plant a tree, have a child, and write a book.

In my case, the last task needs to be qualified: to write a book about *the* book.

I'm a lover of Hispanic civilization. I have written profusely about it. (Too much, perhaps!) Delving into a well of topics, I always come back to a single thought: among the infinite number of items that constitute that civilization, one alone holds its clues, its essence, the blueprint of its DNA: *El Quijote.* Everything begins and ends with it.

All my life I have said to myself, No later than when you turn fifty, you must write about Don Quixote and Sancho. It is a challenge you *must* meet.

In all honesty, despite having justified it to myself in countless ways, as I've done in the preceding pages, I still don't know why I keep rereading this novel. With very rare exceptions, I really don't like reading long novels. I lose patience; my attention wanders. I particularly dislike psychological novels because of the way they defy logic (*Crime and Punishment,* ouch!). I'm allergic to social narratives with a yen for romance (ay, how can the attraction between Heathcliff and Catherine Earnshaw be so destructive?). And I stay away from anything that looks like stream of consciousness (thanks, Clarissa, but I do not do suicide parties!).

I already hear someone saying in the background, "A literary critic who doesn't like novels. I told you so. . . . The horror! The horror!"

Except *El Quijote.*

So I built a shrine for it. I started to buy all sorts of specimens, old and new, traditional and cutting-edge. I have translations into Nahuatl, Yiddish, Swahili, and Korean. I have collectors' editions of Gustave Doré's engravings. I have a first edition of María Amparo Ruiz de Burton's stage adaptation *Don Quixote de la Mancha: A Comedy in Five Acts: Taken From Cervantes' Novel of That Name* of 1876. I have an early paperback of François Filleau de Saint-Martin's incomplete French translation, *Histoire de l'admirable Don Quichotte de la Manche*. And a volume with all of Borges's musings on Cervantes.

By carefully organizing my Quixote volumes on the shelves, I can make a map of my intellectual associations. In its heyday, my collection had close to five hundred books. But the whole endeavor became burdensome. There are never enough shelves. In the First Part, chapter XVII, Sancho offers Don Quixote a wise piece of advice: "I hate keeping things long, and I do not want them to grow rotten with me from over-keeping." I have thought of getting rid of my shrine. But I can't.

"You're just a poser, Ilan, an impostor." A close friend of mine says my fascination with *El Quijote* is a cliché. "You actually don't like *Don Quixote*, let alone love it. You simply want to be associated with it."

Maybe he is right. Not long ago, more than halfway through the completion of the manuscript of this book, I had a dream of Cervantes. The dream was made of two scenes, one short, one long. I must have had the dream in the early morning hours, just before I was about to get up, because those are the dreams I remember most vividly.

In the first scene, Cervantes was first sitting next to me in a large studio with wooden floors. He had thick makeup on his face. His mustache and beard looked fake. He was wearing King Philip II clothes. I had the feeling he was a cheap Shakespearean actor. In fact, he reminded me of the Russian Yiddish actor Shloyme Mikhoels playing *King Lear*.

And he smiled all the time.

We had a conversation. It must have been in Spanish, although in my dreams, whenever people talk, I know what they are saying but I don't hear their words.

He said, "*Soy tu prisionero*," I'm your prisoner. I didn't understand what he meant.

The second scene was at a hotel in what looked like a university campus. I was in my room with my wife. A sealed envelope arrived under the door. The letter inside said the topic of the lecture I was about to deliver needed to be changed. I would instead be having a public conversation with Cervantes.

I was upset, but I told my wife it was fine to change the topic. Then she and I left the room and began to run toward the campus cafeteria. As we approached it, a number of students began doing pirouettes around us. This is a circus, I thought to myself.

Next I was sitting onstage with Cervantes. The auditorium was packed. Each of us had his own chair with a microphone in front. A small table with two glasses of water separated us.

I said, "I'm your prisoner now."

He replied, "*Sí, lo sé.*"

Don Quixote marionette by Tony Sinnett.

CHRONOLOGY

The echoes of *El Quijote* are infinite. This inventory highlights the most influential contributions worldwide. A small fraction is mentioned in this book.

1547 Miguel de Cervantes Saavedra is born in Alcalá de Henares, near Madrid, Spain.

1605 The First Part of *El ingenioso hidalgo don Quijote de la Mancha,* by Cervantes, is published.

1608 César Oudin renders Cervantes's novella *The Ill-Conceived Curiosity* into French. Oudin will translate the First Part of *El Quijote* in 1614. His translation of the Second Part, which completed the rendition of the novel into French, appeared in 1618.

1612 Thomas Shelton releases in London an English-language rendition of *El Quijote,* First Part. It is the first translation of Cervantes's novel ever to be done. Thousands of translations will follow into every single standardized tongue as well as into dialects, jargons, and slangs. It supposedly took Shelton over a month in 1607 to finish his rendition, but he didn't publish it until some five years later.

1613 *The History of Cardenio*, a lost play by William Shakespeare and John Fletcher, is written. It shares with *El Quijote* the character of Cardenio, a nobleman in love who becomes mad and does penance in the Sierra Morena.

1614 A fake sequel to *El Quijote*, under the title of *Segundo tomo del ingenioso hidalgo don Quijote de la Mancha*, written by one Alonso Fernández de Avellaneda, appears in Spain. Cervantes is furious. He uses the excuse to finish his own sequel. Avellaneda's identity remains unknown.

1615 Cervantes's own sequel, known as the Second Part, is published.

1616 Cervantes dies at the age of sixty-eight in Madrid. He is buried in the Convent of the Barefoot Trinitarians.

1622 Lorenzo Franciosini translates the First Part of the novel into Italian. The Second Part will appear in 1625.

1677 François Filleau de Saint-Martin translates *El Quijote* into French as *Histoire de l'admirable Don Quichotte de la Manche*. He leaves the last chapter out in order to write a sequel of his own. He will die before finishing the task. One of Filleau de Saint-Martin's students, Robert Challe, will complete it years later.

1700 French-born English author, playwright, and translator Peter Anthony Motteux renders Cervantes's novel into English. In abbreviated, recomposed, and modified versions, his remains the most frequently reprinted rendition.

1734 *Don Quixote in England*, a play by English satirist Henry Fielding, is staged. It is designed as an attack on Prime Minister Robert Walpole.

1737 For the first time, the words *Quixote*, *Quixotada*, and *Quixotería* enter a lexicon. They are included in Spain's *Diccionario de autoridades*.

1742 In the title page of *Joseph Andrews*, Fielding notes that the novel is "written in Imitation of the Manner of Cervantes, Author of *Don Quixote*." Three years after his death, the translation of *El Quijote* by Irish portrait painter and art collector Charles Jervas (misspelled in the title page as "Jarvis," a typo forever stuck to the name) appears posthumously. It is considered the most accurate but is also described as stiff and without humor. It is reprinted frequently in the eighteenth century.

1752　*The Female Quixote: or, The Adventures of Arabella*, a novel by Gibraltar-born, British poet and actress Charlotte Lennox, is published in England.

1755　After several publication delays, Scottish novelist Tobias Smollett releases in London his own translation of *El Quijote*, known as *The History and Adventures of the Renowned Don Quixote*. He is immediately accused of not knowing a word of Spanish, and his translation is criticized as being a commissioned job wholly done by a group of hired translators who plagiarized portions from previous versions.

1759　The character of Uncle Toby in *The Life and Opinions of Tristram Shandy, Gentleman*, by Anglo-Irish novelist Laurence Sterne, is based on *Don Quixote*.

1761　German baroque composer Georg Philipp Telemann writes the opera *Don Quichotte auf der Hochzeit des Camacho*.

1767　Telemann writes the orchestral suite *Don Quichotte*.

1769　N. Osipov translates *El Quijote* into Russian for the first time. His rendition is based on the French version by Filleau de Saint-Martin.

1780　The first map of Don Quixote's itinerary in La Mancha is drawn by Spanish royal geographer Tomás López. It is endorsed by the *Real Academia Española (RAE)*.

1792　American writer and Pennsylvania Supreme Court justice Hugh Henry Brackenridge publishes the first two parts of his novel *Modern Chivalry: Containing the Adventures of Captain John Farrago and Teague O'Regan, His servant*, set on the western Pennsylvania frontier. The third part appeared in 1793 and the fourth and last in 1797. A revised edition was in 1833.

1801　New Hampshire–based American writer Tabitha Gilman Tenney writes the novel *Female Quixotism, Exhibited in the Romantic Opinions and Extravagant Adventures of Dorcasina Sheldon*.

1833　Mariano Arévalo's five-volume edition appears in Mexico City, the first time *El Quijote* is printed in the New World. At the same time in

Spain, scholar and diplomat Diego Clemencín puts out the first annotated edition of *El Quijote*. His exhaustive effort concludes in 1939.

1838 Konstantin Massal'skii translates *Don Quixote* into Russian. It is the
first translation into that language done from the Spanish.

1850 French artist Honoré Daumier exhibits at the Paris Salon, the official
art exhibition of the Académie des Beaux-Arts in Paris, a series of
drawings based on *El Quijote*.

1851 American writer Herman Melville publishes *Moby-Dick: or, The Whale*.
It displays a strong quixotic quality, the result of Melville's lifelong
admiration of Cervantes's book.

1856 French novelist Gustave Flaubert releases *Madame Bovary*. The book
comes after years of rereading *El Quijote*.

1860 Russian novelist and playwright Ivan Turgenev lectures on *Hamlet*
and *El Quijote* in different parts of Russia.

1863 French engraver, illustrator, and sculptor Gustave Doré completes
the engravings that illustrate the French translation by Louis Viardot in two volumes, published under the aegis of Hachette and Co., in
Paris, and Cassell and Co., in London.

1868 Russian novelist Fyodor Dostoyevsky serializes *The Idiot* in the perio-
dical *The Russian Messenger*. Its protagonist, Prince Myshkin, is an
idealized version of Don Quixote. The serialization concludes in 1869.

1869 The ballet *Don Quixote*, with music by Austrian composer Ludwig
Minkus and choreography by French ballet dancer Marius Petipa, is
presented at the Bolshoi Theatre, in Moscow. Petipa and Minkus will
expand it into five acts in 1871, when it will be staged at the Bolshoi
Kamenny Theatre, in St. Petersburg.

1871 For the next decade, Austrian neurologist and founder of psychoanalysis Sigmund Freud corresponds with his Romanian friend Eduard
Silberstein. They sign their letters as Cipión (Freud) and Berganza
(Silberstein), after the characters of Cervantes's novella *The Colloquy
of the Dogs*.

1874 *Don Quichotte*, a play by French dramatist Victorien Sardou, with
music by the Prussian-born French composer Jacques Offenbach,
premieres in Paris.

1876 Mexican American writer María Amparo Ruiz de Burton, author of the classic novel *The Squatter and the Don*, about land claims in California after the Treaty of Guadalupe Hidalgo in 1848, brings out her theatrical adaptation *Don Quixote de la Mancha: A Comedy in Five Acts: Taken From Cervantes' Novel of That Name*.

1878 Minsk-born writer and pedagogue Sholem Yankev Abramovitch, also known by the name Mendele Mokher Sforim, the grandfather of Yiddish literature, writes the novel *Kitser masoes Binyomen hashlishi*. It is structured as a tribute to Cervantes's book. American journalist, romantic poet, and editor of the *New York Evening Post* William Cullen Bryant writes a poem about Cervantes to commemorate his death.

1884 American writer and humorist Mark Twain publishes *Adventures of Huckleberry Finn*. Along with its prequel, *The Adventures of Tom Sawyer*, it meditates on the themes of *El Quijote*.

1885 British translator John Ormsby publishes his rendition of *El Quijote*, the most scholarly up until then. It is the first translation to become available on the Internet. American poet James Russell Lowell delivers a lecture on *El Quijote* in London's Working Men's College.

1892 British scholar James Fitzmaurice-Kelly publishes the biography *The Life of Miguel de Cervantes Saavedra*.

1895 American writer William Dean Howells, in his book *My Literary Passions*, discusses his discovery of *El Quijote*. Johann Wolfgang von Goethe publishes *Wilhelm Meister's Apprenticeship*, about a journey of self-realization that is inspired by *El Quijote*.

1897 Later-Romantic German composer Richard Strauss writes *Phantastische Variationen über ein Thema ritterlichen Charakters* (Fantastic Variations on a Theme of Knightly Character), Opus 35, on a theme of knightly character. Spanish writer and diplomat Ángel Ganivet publishes *Idearium español* and *El porvenir de España*. They discuss his country's infatuation with *Quijotismo*.

1900 Uruguayan literary critic and cultural commentator José Enrique Rodó publishes his book-long essay *Ariel*, structured as a letter to the youth of Hispanic America. It is an overt variation on Quixote themes.

1902 The French silent movie *Don Quichotte*, by directors Ferdinand Zecca and Lucien Nonguet, is the first ever to be based on *El Quijote*. Spanish *zarzuela* composer Ruperto Chapí premieres the light comedy *La venta de Don Quijote*.

1905 To commemorate the 300th anniversary of the publication of *El Quijote*, Nicaraguan poet and leader of the *Modernista* movement Rubén Darío publishes the poem "*Letanía de nuestro señor Don Quijote*." Spanish philosopher and novelist Miguel de Unamuno releases his volume *Vida de Don Quijote y Sancho*. James Fitzmaurice-Kelly publishes *Cervantes in England*. José Martínez Ruíz, better known as Azorín, commissioned by the newspaper *El Imparcial*, follows the route of Don Quixote in Spain, writing a travel book that is also a psychological exploration of the novel's impact in the nation's popular imagination.

1907 Mexican lampooner José Guadalupe Posada engraves the *Calavera Quijotesca*.

1909 French composer Jules Massenet begins composing his five-act opera, *Don Quichotte*, with a libretto by French librettist Henri Caïn. Massenet calls it a "*comédie-héroïque*."

1912 Russian Jewish poet of the Hebrew literary renaissance Chaim Nachman Bialik translates *El Quijote* into Hebrew. His source is a Russian version.

1914 Spanish thinker and cultural commentator José Ortega y Gasset writes *Meditaciones del Quijote*.

1915 American actor, singer, and comedian William DeWolf Hopper produces the short film *Don Quixote*.

1916 Fitzmaurice-Kelly publishes *Cervantes and Shakespeare*.

1922 Spanish composer Manuel de Falla's *El retablo de maese Pedro*, a puppet-opera in one act, with a prologue and an epilogue, has its premiere.

1926 Spanish theorist, literary critic, and journalist Ramiro de Maeztu publishes *Don Quijote, Don Juan y la Celestina*, in which he meditated on Spain's archetypal literary character.

1927 British detective writer, biographer, and polemicist G. K. Chesterton writes *The Return of Don Quixote*.

1928   Daniel Venegas serializes his Chicano novel, *The Adventures of Don Chipote: or, A Sucker's Tale*, in the Mexican newspaper *El Heraldo*. It tells the quixotic story of an impoverished and illiterate peasant who emigrates to the United States.

1931   Hasidic parable "Die Wahrheit über Sancho Panza," by German-language Czech novelist and insurance worker Franz Kafka, appears in the collection *Beim Bau der Chinesischen Mauer*.

1932   French composer Maurice Ravel writes the first of three songs for voice and piano, collectively known as *Don Quichotte à Dulcinée*, set to poems on *El Quijote* by French poet, playwright, and diplomat Paul Morand.

1933   Austrian film director Georg Wilhelm Pabst releases the film *Adventures of Don Quixote*. There are three versions of it, all done the same year: one in French, another in English, and the third in German. Russian actor Feodor Chaliapin stars in all of them.

1935   Spanish-born Oxford scholar, historian, and diplomat Salvador de Madariaga releases the literary study *Don Quixote: An Introductory Essay in Psychology*.

1939   Argentine *hombre de letras* Jorge Luis Borges publishes in the magazine Sur his story "Pierre Menard, Author of the *Quixote*." It is reprinted in his 1944 collection, *Ficciones*.

1940   Catalan composer Roberto Gerhard writes the ballet *Don Quixote*. In 1947 Gerhard rewrote the ballet. It is staged at London's Covent Garden with choreography by Irish-born British dancer and choreographer Ninette de Valois and décor by English printmaker Edward Burra.

1945   Catalan surrealist artist Salvador Dalí creates a series of watercolors to illustrate the First Part of *El Quijote*, published by Random House.

1947   The first full-length feature film based on *El Quijote* is released. It is called *Don Quijote de La Mancha*, directed by Spanish screenwriter and director Rafael Gil. Pedro Salinas, a Spanish poet who belonged to the Generation of '27 aesthetic movement, publishes in *The Nation* an essay called "*Don Quixote* and the Novel."

1948   Spanish journalist, translator, and essayist Luis Astrana Marín publishes the first of his seven-volume biography *Vida ejemplar y heróica de Miguel de Cervantes Saavedra*. The last volume appears in 1958. The first partial translation into Japanese based on the Spanish, by Hirosada Nagata, is released in Tokyo.

1949   American translator and scholar of Romance languages Samuel Putnam releases his translation of *El Quijote* into contemporary English. He also rendered into English a couple of novellas from Cervantes's *Exemplary Novellas*.

1950   British translator of European literature J. M. (John Michael) Cohen, also known for his translations of Rousseau, Rabelais, Montaigne, and Teresa de Ávila, renders *El Quijote* into English for Penguin Books.

1951   During the fall semester, Russian-born trilingual novelist Vladimir Nabokov teaches a course at Harvard on *El Quijote*, accusing it of cruelty. The first translation of the novel into Yiddish is released by Argentine Jewish intellectual and newspaper editor Pinie Katz. Done directly from the Spanish, it is published in Buenos Aires.

1953   Avant-garde Irish novelist Samuel Beckett premieres the play *Waiting for Godot* at the Théâtre de Babylone, in Paris. Berlin-born Jewish philologist Erich Auerbach publishes the study *Mimesis: The Representation of Reality in Western Literature*. One of its chapters deals with Dulcinea.

1954   Irish Hispanist Walker Starkie, known for his worldwide travels, publishes his abridged translation of *El Quijote* into English. The unabridged version will appear in 1964.

1955   Spanish scholar Juan Givanel Mas y Gaziel published the illustrated volume *Historia gráfica de Cervantes y del Quijote*. The cover of the French weekly magazine *Les Lettres Françaises* features a silhouette by Spanish artist Pablo Picasso of the knight-errant and his squire. It quickly becomes a staple of the novel's durability. American writer Kenneth Grahame published the novel *Adventures in Yankeeland*, which transposes *Don Quixote* to the United States.

1956   American film director and actor Orson Welles, in *The Frank Sinatra*

Show, comes up with the idea of making a film based on *El Quijote*. This lifelong project will be left unfinished. In 1992, Spanish B-movie director Jesús Franco and producer Patxi Irigoyen made a 116-minute remix, greeted negatively by audiences. The Russian film *Don Kikhot*, directed by Ukrainian-born Russian Jewish director Grigori Kozintsev, wins an award at the Cannes Film Festival.

1961   A collection of vignettes by Puerto Rican activist and New York newspaper columnist Jesús Colón is published under the title *A Puerto Rican in New York and Other Sketches*. It is marked by a quixotic view of immigrant life as dwelling between two extremes: materialism and idealism.

1965   The American musical *Man of La Mancha*, with a book by playwright Dale Wasserman, lyrics by songwriter Joe Darion, and music by composer Mitch Leigh, premieres on Broadway. (American-based British poet W. H. Auden was originally asked to write the libretto, producing an early draft.) The movie adaptation, with Peter O'Toole, Sophia Loren, and Ian Richardson, and directed by Canadian filmmaker Arthur Hiller, is released in 1972. Russian choreographer George Balanchine premieres his ballet *Don Quixote*, with music by Russian-born composer Nicholas Nabokov, and performed by American ballerina Suzanne Farrell. French filmmaker Éric Rohmer makes a twenty-three-minute movie called *Don Quichotte de Cervantes*.

1966   French semiotician Michel Foucault publishes *The Order of Things*, in which *El Quijote*, a central topic, is seen from a semiotic perspective.

1973   Mexican standup comedian Mario Moreno "Cantinflas" is Sancho Panza in the movie *Don Quijote cabalga de nuevo*.

1977   British comedian John Cleese, a guest of *The Muppet Show*, apologizes for not singing the lyrics of "The Impossible Dream," the theme song of *Man of La Mancha*, calling it trash.

1980   The first branch of the Japanese discount store Don Quixote, known as Donki, opens up in the Suginami neighborhood of Tokyo. Japanese anime series *Don Quixote: Tales of La Mancha* is released. British writer Robin Chapman publishes the novel *The Duchess' Diary*. It is part of a trilogy, along with *Sancho's Golden Age* (2004) and *Pasamonte's*

Life (2005), featuring characters from *El Quijote*. Chapman is also the author of *Shakespeare's Don Quixote* (2011), a novel-cum-dialogue between Shakespeare, John Fletcher, and Cervantes.

1982   British novelist and Catholic polemicist Graham Greene publishes the novel *Monsignor Quixote*.

1983   Swiss astronomer Paul Wild discovers Asteroid 3552. It functions as an asteroid but behaves like a comet. He names it Don Quixote.

1985   American experimental writer Kathy Acker writes the novel *Don Quixote: Which Was a Dream*. And Susan Sontag writes an essay on *Don Quixote* for Spain's Tourist Agency. It is called "España: Todo bajo el sol."

1986   Czech novelist Milan Kundera published *The Art of the Novel*, which includes the essay "The Depreciated Legacy of Cervantes."

1987   Dinamic Software releases in Spain the video game *Don Quijote*, based on an animated series produced by Televisión Española.

1991   TVE, Spanish television, produces the movie *El caballero Don Quijote*, based on the First Part, by Spanish screenwriter and director Manuel Gutiérrez Aragón.

1995   Indian-born British writer Salman Rushdie publishes the novel *The Moor's Last Sigh*. American academic Burton Raffel publishes his translation into English of *El Quijote*.

1998   Chilean-born Spanish-based novelist Roberto Bolaño publishes the novel *The Savage Detectives*. Terry Gilliam, the American-born British comedian and director, fails to make a movie called *The Man Who Killed Don Quixote*, with Jean Rochefort and Johnny Depp. After being postponed, it went into production in 2000, with a budget of $32.1 million. The effort collapsed after a number of mishaps, including insurance issues, the destruction of equipment during a flood, and an actor's illness. Apparently, the project acquired new life and—with a different script—was slated to be completed for a 2015 release.

2000   American film director Peter Yates makes the TV movie *Don Quixote*. The script is by British novelist John Mortimer. It stars John Lithgow, Bob Hoskins, and Isabella Rossellini.

2002 Mexican-born American literary critic and cultural commentator Ilan Stavans publishes a Spanglish translation of *El Quijote*, First Part, chapter I, in a literary supplement in Barcelona. It is included in his book *Spanglish: The Making of a New American Language*. TVE produces *El caballero Don Quijote*, a movie based only on the Second Part and directed by Gutiérrez Aragón. The documentary *Lost in La Mancha*, directed by Keith Fulton and Louis Pepe, is released. It is about Terry Gilliam's failed attempt to freely adapt, or pay tribute to, *El Quijote* in the movie called *The Man Who Killed Don Quixote*.

2003 American translator Edith Grossman is the first woman ever to translate *El Quijote* into English.

2005 The Royal Academy of the Spanish Language in Madrid releases a commemorative edition of *El Quijote* to celebrate the 400th anniversary of its release.

2006 Peruvian scholar Demetrio Túpac Yupanqui translates parts of *El Quijote* into Quechua.

2007 The Conseil de l'Europe, an organization endowed with promoting Europe's cultural heritage, gives its official stamp to the tourist route the knight-errant and his squire supposedly follow in their three adventures. A Spanish CGI-animated movie *Donkey Xote*, with Sancho's donkey as lead character, is released.

2009 Retired American university librarian James H. Montgomery published *Don Quixote*. It is the twentieth full rendition of the novel into English.

2015 To relocate them in a more decorous grave, the purported remains of Cervantes, along with those of his wife of thirty years, Catalina de Salazar, identified through DNA, are exhumed in the Convent of the Barefoot Trinitarians in Madrid. The publication of the Second Part of *El Quijote* turns four hundred years old, acknowledged with symposia, translations, books, and film cycles.

2016 The 400th anniversary of the death of Shakespeare and Cervantes, the two most important writers of the Renaissance, is commemorated globally.

CREDITS

© 2014 Estate of Pablo Picasso / Artists CREDIT: Rights Society (ARS), New York / Private Collection / Peter Willi / Bridgeman Images

PAGE 94   Monument to Don Quixote and Sancho in Plaza de España, Madrid. John Greim/LightRocket/Getty Images

PAGE 99   *The Skulls of Don Quixote*, c.1910–13, printed 1943 (photo-relief etching with engraving), Posada, José Guadalupe (1851–1913) / Museum of Fine Arts, Houston, Texas, USA / gift of the Friends of Freda Radoff. / Bridgeman Images

PAGE 120   *Don Quixote and the Windmills*, by Salvador Dalí. © Salvador Dalí, Fundació Gala-Salvador Dalí, Artists Rights Society (ARS), New York 2014

PAGE 122   *Don Quixote and the Windmills*, from *Don Quixote de la Mancha* by Miguel Cervantes (1547–1616) engraved by Heliodore Joseph Pisan (1822–90) (engraving) (b/w photo) (see also 141799), Doré, Gustave (1832–83) (after) / Bibliothèque Nationale, Paris, France / Bridgeman Images

PAGE 161   *Quixote and Rocinante* by Barry Moser. Used by permission of the artist

PAGE 165   Movie poster of *Lost in La Mancha* (2002), directed by Keith Fulton and Louis Pepe. Courtesy of Moviestore collection Ltd / Alamy

PAGE 167   Poster for the musical *Man of La Mancha*. © The Al Hirschfeld Foundation. www.AlHirschfeldFoundation.org. Al Hirschfeld is also represented by the Margo Feiden Galleries Ltd., New York

PAGE 169   *Don Quixote en Spanglish*. With permission of David Enriquez and Ilan Stavans

PAGE 175   Title page of the French translation by Francois Filleau de Saint-Martin. Image courtesy of the Cervantes Project, Textual Iconography of the Quixote Digital Archive, Texas A&M University Libraries (dqi.tamu.edu)

PAGE 211   Don Quixote marionette by Tony Sinnett, www.tonysinnett.com

THROUGHOUT   Details of the Don Quixote chess set courtesy of The Chess House, www.chesshouse.com

ACKNOWLEDGMENTS

Such is my lifelong obsession with this subject that it feels as if it has taken me more than four hundred years to write *Quixote*—since the First Part debuted in 1605.

At Norton, my heartfelt gracias to Alane Salierno Mason, whose passion for translation of world literature is a touchstone benefiting us all, and who saw the seed for this volume in 2001, upon reading a special issue of *Hopscotch: A Cultural Review*. I cherish her friendship as well as her savvy, intelligent editorial touch. I wrote a first version of this book, and upon completion, I understood, in conversation with her, that it was the wrong book. So I rewrote it from scratch.

Denise Scarfi, at one time Alane Mason's editorial assistant and now a school teacher at a Spanish-English dual-language school in the Bronx, meticulously read the second version of the manuscript, graciously offering her insights. Mary Babcock did an exemplary copy-editing job. Kay Banning was in charge of the index.

Thanks to my tireless Amherst College assistant, Mariela Figueroa, for the countless ways in which she helped bring this volume together. My former student Irina Troconis, who went on various research missions, was

228

ACKNOWLEDGMENTS

also an invaluable resource. And I benefited from the help of four other assistants: Derek García, Rebecca Pol, Heather Richard, and Federico Sucre.

The Cervantes industry has been a topic of mine for years. It's impossible to thank the countless people with whom I have engaged in conversation, real and imaginary. Among them are Paula Abate, Jennifer Acker, Verónica Albin, Lalo Alcaraz, Frederick Aldama, Rene Alegría, John Alexander, Frederick de Armas, Diana de Armas Wilson, Harold Augenbraum, David Bellos, Silvia Betti, Harold Bloom, Sara Brenneis, William P. Childers, Uri Cohen, Isabel Durán, Eko, Laszlo Erdelyi, Marcela García, Matthew Glassman, Erica González, Roberto González Echevarría, Jorge E. C. Gracia, Edith Grossman, Iván Jaksić, Steven G. Kellman, Stacy Klein, Tom Lathrop, Jeffrey Lawrence, Chris Lovett, Luis Loya, Victoria Maillo, James Maraniss, Roberto Márquez, Juan Carlos Marset, Juan Fernando Merino, Rogelio Miñana, María Negroni, Glenda Nieto, Eliezer Nowodworski, Maibe Ponet, Burton Raffel, Nieves Romero-Díaz, David G. Roskies, Elda Rotor, Nina Scott, Steve Sheinkin, Earl Shorris, Ilene Smith, Gonzalo Sobejano, Neal Sokol, Patricio Tapia, Peter Temes, Carlos Uriona, Julio Vélez-Sainz, Juan Villoro, David Ward, Aline White, Kurt Wildermuth, Karen Winkler, Martín Felipe Yriart, Pablo Zinger, and Raúl Zurita.

Finally, the extraordinary people of Restless Books—Annette Hochstein, Joshua Ellison, Michael Berk, Nathan Rostron, Jack Saul, Brinda Ayer, Alex Sarrigeorgiou, and Renata Limón—allowed me the opportunity to delve into the topic with their full support. I am in their debt.

SOURCES

The most authoritative Spanish edition is *Don Quijote de la Mancha*, Edición del Instituto Cervantes, edited by Francisco Rico (2 vols.; Barcelona: Instituto Cervantes-Crítica, 1998).

In English, my *ur*-text, from which I quote, is the John Ormsby translation of *Don Quixote*, first published in London in 1885 and available at http://www.gutenberg.org/ebooks/996. Occasionally I also employ *Don Quixote de La Mancha*, translated by Samuel Putnam (New York: Viking, 1949), with an introduction and critical text based on the first editions of 1605 and 1615, as well as variorum notes. And *The Complete Works of Miguel de Cervantes Saavedra*, edited by James Fitzmaurice-Kelly (Glasgow: Gowans & Gray, 1901–3).

I have also made ample use of various resources: Juan Bautista de Avalle-Arce, *Enciclopedia cervantina* (Alcalá de Henares, Spain: Centro de Estudios Cervantinos, 1997); Anthony J. Cascardi, editor, *The Cambridge Companion to Cervantes* (Cambridge: Cambridge University Press, 2001); Tom Lathrop, *Don Quijote Dictionary: Spanish-English* (Newark, Delaware: Juan de la Cuesta, 1999); Howard Mancing, *The Cervantes Encyclopedia* (2 vols.; Westport, Connecticut: Greenwood Press, 2004); and Mancing, *Cervantes' Don Quixote: A Reference Guide* (Westport, Connecticut: Greenwood Press, 2006).

SOURCES

At the lexicographic level, I sought Sebastián de Covarrubias Orozco, *Tesoro de la lengua castellana o española*, edited by Felipe C. R. Maldonado, revised by Manuel Camarero (Madrid: Editorial Castalia, 1995); *Diccionario de autoridades* (Madrid: Gredos, 1990); *Historical Thesaurus of the Oxford English Dictionary*, edited by Christian Kay et al. (Oxford: Oxford University Press, 2009); and *Merriam-Webster's Collegiate Dictionary* (Springfield, Massachusetts: Merriam-Webster, 2011).

Finally, in structure as well as scope, the immediate ancestor of this book, in my own work, is *Imagining Columbus: A Literary Voyage* (New York: Macmillan, 1992).

The following are the basic bibliographical resources connected with each of the chapters. Entries are listed in the first chapter they are cited or mentioned and then not subsequently.

PREFACE

Jorge Luis Borges, "La conducta novelística de Cervantes," in *Cervantes y el Quijote*, edited by Sara Luisa del Carril and Mercedes Rubio de Zocci (Buenos Aires: Emecé, 2005), pp. 17–22; Charles-Augustin Sainte-Beuve, *The Literary Criticism of Sainte-Beuve*, edited and translated by Emerson R. Marks (Lincoln: University of Nebraska Press, 1971); Solar System Dynamics, Jet Propulsion Laboratory, http://ssd.jpl.nasa.gov; Ilan Stavans, "A Rejection Letter," *New Republic*, online, February 10, 2005, reprinted in *"Don Quixote* at Four Hundred," in *A Critic's Journey* (Ann Arbor: University of Michigan Press, 2010), pp. 95–100; Ilan Stavans, "The Downside of Digging Up Cervantes," *The New Yorker* online, March 19, 2015; and Lionel Trilling, "Manners, Morals, and the Novel," in *The Moral Obligation to Be Intelligent: Selected Essays*, edited by Leon Wieseltier (New York: Farrar, Straus & Giroux, 2000), pp. 105–9.

1 | IN HIS LIKENESS

Luis Astrana Marín, *Vida ejemplar y heróica de Miguel de Cervantes Saavedra* (Madrid: Instituto Editorial Reus, 1948–58); William Byron, *Cervantes: A*

Biography (Garden City, New York: Doubleday, 1978); Jean Canavaggio, *Cervantes*, translated by J. R. Jones (New York: W. W. Norton, 1991); Miguel de Cervantes, *Exemplary Novellas*, translated by Walter K. Kelly (Emmaus, Pennsylvania: Sory Classics, 1952); Daniel Eisenberg, *A Study of Don Quixote*, preface by Richard Bjornson (Newark, Delaware: Juan de la Cuesta, 1987); Manuel Fernández Álvarez, *Cervantes visto por un historiador* (Madrid: Espasa, 2005); James Fitzmaurice-Kelly, *Life of Miguel de Cervantes Saavedra* (London: Chapman & Hall, 1892); Stephen Gilman, *The Novel according to Cervantes* (Berkeley: University of California Press, 1989); Roberto González-Echevarría, editor, *Cervantes' Don Quixote: A Casebook* (Oxford: Oxford University Press, 2005); Juan Givanel Mas y Gaziel, *Historia gráfica de Cervantes y del Quijote* (Madrid: Editorial Plus-Ultra, 1955); Vladimir Nabokov, *Lectures on Don Quixote*, edited by Fredson Bowers (New York: Harcourt Brace, 1983); and Charles D. Presberg, *Adventures in Paradox: "Don Quixote" and the Western Tradition* (University Park: Pennsylvania State University Press, 2001).

2 | THE SO-CALLED NORMAL

John Jay Allen, "El desarrollo de Dulcinea y la evolución de don Quijote," *Nueva revista de filología hispánica*, 38 (1990): 849–56; Diana de Armas Wilson, "Rethinking Cervantine Utopias: Some No (Good) Places in Renaissance England and Spain," in *Echoes and Inscriptions: Comparative Approaches to Early Modern Spanish Literatures*, edited by Barbara A. Simerka and Christopher B. Weimer (Lewisburg, Pennsylvania: Bucknell University Press, 2000), pp. 191–209; Erich Auerbach, "The Enchanted Dulcinea," in *Mimesis: The Representation of Reality in Western Literature*, translated by Willard R. Trask (Princeton, New Jersey: Princeton University Press, 1953); María del Carmen Cañizares Ruíz, "La 'ruta de *Don Quijote*' en Castilla, La Mancha: nuevo itinerario cultural europeo," *Nimbus: revista de climatología, meteorología y paisaje*, 21–22 (2008): 55–75; Arthur Efron, *Don Quixote and the Dulcinated World* (Austin: University of Texas Press, 1971); Ruth El Saffar, *Beyond Fiction: The Recovery of the Feminine in the Novels of Cervantes* (Berkeley: University of California Press, 1984); Joseph R. Jones, "The Baratarian

Archipelago: Cheap Isle, Chicanery Isle, Joker's Isle," in *"Ingeniosa Invención": Essays on Golden Age Spanish Literature for Geoffrey L. Stagg in Honor of His Eighty-Fifth Birthday*, edited by Ellen M. Anderson and Amy R. Williamsen (Newark, Delaware: Juan de la Cuesta, 1999), pp. 137–47; Salvador de Madariaga, *Don Quixote: An Introductory Essay in Psychology* (Oxford: Oxford University Press, 1935); Alberto Manguel and Gianni Guadalupi, *The Dictionary of Imaginary Places*, updated edition (New York: Harcourt Brace, 1980); Haruki Murakami, *Norwegian Wood*, translated by Jay Rubin (New York: Alfred A. Knopf, 1999); Lionel Trilling, *The Liberal Imagination: Essays on Literature and Society*, introduction by Louis Menand (New York: New York Review of Books, 2008); John Updike, "In Response to a Request from *Le Nouvelle Observateur* to Write Something about Cervantes' *Don Quixote*," in *More Matter: Essays and Criticism* (New York: Alfred A. Knopf, 1983), pp. 844–46; Mario J. Valdés, "*Don Quijote de la Mancha* y la verdad de Dulcinea del Toboso," *Revista canadiense de estudios hispánicos*, 25 (2000): 29–41; and Eric J. Ziolkowski, "Don Quijote's Windmill and Fortune's Will," *Modern Language Review*, 86 (1991): 884–97.

3 | MADNESS AND METHOD

Josep Béa and Victor Hernández, "Don Quixote: Freud and Cervantes," *International Journal of Psychoanalysis*, 65 (1984): 141–53; Aubrey F. G. Bell, "The Wisdom of Don Quixote," *Books Abroad*, 21, no. 3 (1947): 259–63; Walter Benjamin, "The Storyteller: Observations on the Works of Nikolai Leskov," in *Selected Writings*, Vol. 3: *1935–1938*, translated by Edmund Jephcott et al., edited by Howard Eiland and Michael W. Jennings (Cambridge, Massachusetts: Harvard University Press, 1999), pp. 143–66; Anne J. Cruz, "Psyche and Gender in Cervantes," in *The Cambridge Companion to Cervantes*, edited by Anthony J. Cascardi (Cambridge: Cambridge University Press, 2002); Helen Deutsch, "Don Quixote and Don Quixotism," in *Neuroses and Character Types: Clinical Psychoanalytic Studies* (New York: International University Press, 1965); Ruth Anthony El Saffar and Diana de Armas Wilson, editors, *Quixotic Desire: Psychoanalytic Perspectives on Cervantes* (Ithaca, New York: Cornell University Press, 1993); Henry Fielding, *Joseph Andrews* and *Sha-*

mela, edited by Judith Hawley (New York: Penguin Classics, 1999); Fielding, *Rape upon Rape; or, The Justice Caught in His Own Trap and The Coffee-House Politician* (1730), Woodson Research Center, Fondren Library, Rice University, http://exhibits.library.rice.edu/items/show/640; Michel Foucault, *The Order of Things: An Archaeology of the Human Sciences*, translated by Alan Sheridan-Smith (New York: Random House, 1970); Sigmund Freud, *Complete Works* (7 vols.; New York: Penguin, 2003); Joan E. Gedo and Ernest S. Wolf, "Freud's Novelas Ejemplares," *Annual of Psychoanalysis*, 1 (1973): 299–317; Léon Grinberg and Juan Francisco Rodríguez, "The Influence of Cervantes on the Future Creator of Psychoanalysis," *International Journal of Psychoanalysis*, 65 (1984): 155–68; Iván Jaksić, "Don Quijote's Encounter with Technology," *Cervantes*, 14, no. 1 (1994): 75–95; Carroll B. Johnson, *Madness and Lust: A Psychoanalytical Approach to Don Quixote* (Berkeley: University of Califlornia Press, 1983); Jacques Lacan, *Écrits* (Paris: Éditions du Seuil, 1966); György Lukács, *The Theory of the Novel*, translated by Anna Bostock (London: Merlin Press, 1971); V. C. Pando, "The Wolf's Men: The Relationship between Freud and Cervantes," *Psicopatología*, 26, nos. 1/2 (2006): 33–60; James A. Parr, "Cervantes Foreshadows Freud: On Don Quixote's Flight from the Feminine and the Physical," *Cervantes: Bulletin of the Cervantes Society of America*, 15, no. 2 (1995): 16–25; S. S. Prawer, "The Dog, the Knight, and the Squire Sigmund Freud's Reading of Cervantes," *Oxford German Studies*, 37, no. 1 (2008): 74–91; E. C. Riley, "Cervantes, Freud, and Psychoanalytic Narrative Theory," *Modern Language Review*, 88, no. 1 (1993): 1–14; Theodore Sarbin, "The Quixotic Principle: A Belletristic Approach to the Psychological Study of Imaginings and Believings," in *The Social Context of Conduct: Psychological Writings of Theodore Sarbin*, edited by Vernon L. Allen and Karl E. Scheibe (New York: Praeger, 1982), pp. 169–86; and Henry W. Sullivan, "Don Quixote de la Mancha: Analyzable or Unanalyzable?," *Cervantes: Bulletin of the Cervantes Society of America*, 18, no. 1 (1998): 4–23.

4 | A MODERN NOVEL

John Jay Allen, "The Narrators, the Reader, and Don Quijote," *MLN*, 91 (1976): 201–12; Diana de Armas Wilson, *Cervantes, the Novel, and the New*

World (Oxford: Oxford University Press, 2000); Edward T. Aylward, *Towards a Revaluation of Avellaneda's False "Quijote"* (Newark, Delaware: Juan de la Cuesta, 1989); Harold Bloom, editor, *Cervantes* (New York: Chelsea House, 1987); Jorges Luis Borges, *Discusión* (Buenos Aires: Alianza, 1997), pp. 3–4; Borges, "Partial Magic of the *Quijote*," translated by James E. Irby, in *Labyrinths*, edited by Donald A. Yates and James E. Irby (New York: New Directions, 1962), pp. 193–96; Borges, "The Wall and the Books," in *The Perpetuan Race of Achille and the Tortoise*, translated by Esther Allen, Suzanne Jill Levine, and Eliot Weinberger (London: Penguin Books, 2010), pp. 78–81; Américo Castro, *Cervantes y los casticismos españoles* (Madrid: Alianza Editorial, 1966); Samuel Taylor Coleridge, *Coleridge's Poetry and Prose: Authoritative Texts and Criticism*, selected and edited by Nicholas Halmi, Paul Magnuson, and Raimonda Modiano (New York: W. W. Norton, 2004); Anne J. Cruz and Carroll B. Johnson, editors, *Cervantes and His Postmodern Constituencies* (New York: Garland, 1999); Daniel Eisenberg, *Cervantes y el Quijote* (Barcelona: Montesinos, 1993); Stephen Gilman, *Cervantes y Avellaneda: estudio de una imitación*, translated by Margit Frenk Alatorre (Mexico City: Colegio de México, 1951); Paul Groussac, *Un énigme litterarire: le D. Quichotte d'Avellaneda* (Paris: A. Picard, 1903); James Iffland, *De fiestas y aguafiestas: risa, locura e ideología en Cervantes y Avellaneda* (Madrid: Iberoamericana, 1999); Maureen Ihrie, *Skepticism in Cervantes* (London: Tamesis Books, 1982); Milan Kundera, *The Art of the Novel*, translated by Linda Asher (New York: Grove Press, 1986); Harry Levin, *Contexts of Criticism* (Cambridge, Massachusetts: Harvard University Press, 1957); Ellen Lokos, "The Politics of Identity and the Enigma of Cervantine Genealogy," in *Cervantes and His Postmodern Constituencies*, edited by Anne J. Cruz and Carroll B. Johnson (New York: Garland, 1999); Leopoldo Lugones, *El imperio jesuítico: ensayo histórico* [1907] (Buenos Aires: Losada, 1959); Jesús G. Maeso, "El sistema narrativo del Quijote: la construcción del personaje Cid Hamete Benengeli," *Cervantes*, 15, no. 1 (1995): 111–41; Howard Mancing, *The Chivalric World of Don Quixote: Style, Structure, and Narrative Technique* (Columbia: University of Missouri Press, 1982); José Ortega y Gasset, *Meditations on Quixote*, translated by Evelyn Rugg and Diego Marín (New York: W. W. Norton, 1961); Ortega y Gasset, *The Revolt of the Masses* (New York: W. W. Norton,

1994); Felipe Pérez Capo, *El "Quijote" en el teatro: repertorio croinológico de 290 producciones relacionadas con la inmortal obra de Cervantes* (Barcelona: Millá, 1947); Geoffrey Stagg, "El sabio Cide Hamete Benengeli," *Bulletin of Hispanic Studies*, 33 (1956): 218–25; and Ilan Stavans and Iván Jaksić, *What Is 'la hispanidad'?* (Austin: University of Texas Press, 2011).

5 | THE CONJUROR OF WORDS

Amado Alonso, *Castellano, español, idioma nacional: historia espiritual de tres nombres* (Buenos Aires: Losada, 1938); Ambrose Bierce, *The Devil's Dictionary* (New York: Dover, 1993); Jorge Luis Borges, *El idioma de los argentinos* [1928] (Buenos Aires: Alianza, 2001); Borges, "An Investigation of the Word," translated by Suzanne Jill Levine and Eliot Weinberger, in *Selected Non-Fiction*, edited by Eliot Weinberger (New York: Viking, 1999), pp. 32–39; Miguel de Cervantes, *Don Quijote: A New Translation*, translated by Burton Raffel, introduction by Diana de Armas Wilson (New York: W. W. Norton, 1999); *Diccionario de la lengua española* (Barcelona: Espasa-Calpe, 2001); Paul Groussac, *Crítica literaria* (Buenos Aires: J. Menéndez e hijo, 1924); Franz Kafka, *Die Verwandlung* (Leipzig: Kurt Wolf, 1915); Kafka, *Selected Short Stories*, translated by Willa and Edwin Muir, introduction by Philip Rahv (New York: Modern Library, 1993); Samuel Johnson, *Selected Essays*, edited by David Womersley (New York: Penguin Classics, 2003); Rafael Lapesa, *Historia de la lengua española*, 9th edition, prologue by Ramón Menéndez Pidal (Madrid: Gredos, 1981); Ángel Rosenblat, *La lengua del "Quijote"* (Madrid: Gredos, 1971); and Sócrates, "¿Cuántas palabras tiene *Don Quijote*?," *Solosequenosenada*, June 1, 2009, http://www.solosequenosenada.com/2009/06/01/cuantas-palabras-tiene-el-libro-don-quijote-de-la-mancha-de-cervantes/.

Here are two other examples of the first line of *El Quijote* in English translation, organized chronologically by their respective year of publication:

- Thomas Shelton: "There lived not long since, in a certain village of the Mancha, the name whereof I purposely omit, a gentleman of their calling that used to pile up in their halls old lances, halberds, morions, and such other armours and weapons."

SOURCES

- Samuel Putnam: "In a village of La Mancha the name of which I have no desire to recall, there lived not so long ago one of those gentlemen who always have a lance in the rack, an ancient buckler, a skinny nag, and a greyhound for the chase."

6 | *QUIJOTISMO* AND *MENARDISMO*

Sebastian Balfour, *The End of the Spanish Empire: 1898–1923* (Oxford: Clarendon Press, 1997); Jorge Luis Borges, "Pierre Menard, Author of the *Quixote*," in *Labyrinths*, translated by James E. Irby (New York: New Directions, 1964); Carolyn Boyd, *Historia Patria: Politics, History, and National Identity in Spain, 1875–1975* (Princeton, New Jersey: Princeton University Press, 1997); Christopher Britt Arredondo, *Quixotismo: The Imaginative Denial of Spain's Loss of Empire* (Albany: State University of New York Press, 2005); Américo Castro, *El pensamiento de Cervantes*, edited by Julio Rodríguez-Puértolas (Barcelona: Noguer, 1972); Castro, *An Idea of History: Selected Essays*, translated and edited by Stephen Gilman and Edmund L. King (Columbus: Ohio State University Press, 1977); William Childers, *Transnational Cervantes* (Toronto: University of Toronto Press, 2006); John J. Ciofalo, "Goya's Enlightenment Protagonist: A Quixotic Dreamer of Reason," *Eighteenth-Century Studies*, 30, no. 4 (1997): 421–36; Diego Clemencín, editor, *El ingenioso hidalgo don Quijote de la Mancha*, by Miguel de Cervantes, 400th anniversary edition, with 356 engravings by Gustave Doré and critical study by Luis Astrana Marín (Valencia, Spain: Editorial Alfredo Ortells, 1993); Rubén Darío, *Selected Writings*, edited by Ilan Stavans, translated by Greg Simon, Andrew Hurley, and Steven F. White (New York: Penguin, 2005); Isabel Escandell Proust, "Goya, autor de dos imágenes de don Quijote," *Volver a Cervantes: actas del IV Congreso Internacional de la Asociación de Cervantistas*, Lepanto, 1, no. 8 (2001): 415–38; Carlos Fuentes, *Cervantes o la crítica de la lectura* (Mexico: Joaquín Mortíz, 1976); Fuentes, *Myself with Others: Selected Essays* (New York: Farrar, Straus & Giroux, 1990); Ángel Ganivet, *Idearium español, con El porvenir de España* (Madrid: Espasa-Calpe, 1897); Gabriel García Márquez and Roberto Pomb, "Habla Marcos," *Revista Cambio* (March 25, 2001), http://www.elhistoriador.com.ar/entrevistas/m

/marcos.php; Ricardo Gullón, *La invención del 98 y otros ensayos* (Madrid: Gredos, 1969); A. G. Lo Ré, "A Possible Source for Picasso's Drawing of Don Quixote," *Cervantes*, 12, no. 1 (1992): 105–10; Ramiro de Maeztu, *Defensa de la hispanidad* (Madrid: Espasa, 1946); Emmanuel Marigno, "La visión de don Quijote de Francisco Goya, un autoportrait métaphorique?," *Crisoladas: revue du C.R.I.S.O.L.*, 16/17, no. 1 (2006): 162–74; José Martínez Ruiz "Azorín," *La ruta de Don Quijote* (Madrid: Biblioteca Renacimiento, 1915); Manuel V. Monsonís Monfort, "Un Quijote de Picasso," *Ars Longa*, 14–15 (2005–6): 345–54; José Ortega y Gasset, *The Dehumanization of Art and Other Essays on Art, Culture, and Literature* (Princeton, New Jersey: Princeton University Press, 1968); Nicola Palladino, "Pintura, imaginación y deseo. Le Illustrazioni di Dalí al *Don Quijote*," *Central Virtual Cervantes* (2005): 103–26; V. S. Pritchett, *The Myth Makers* (New York: Vintage, 1980); Pritchett, *The Spanish Temper* (London: Chatto & Windus, 1954); José Enrique Rodó, *Ariel*, translation, reader's reference, and annotated bibliography by Margaret Sayers Peden (Austin: University of Texas Press, 1988); Rachel Schmidt, "Conclusion: Goya and the Romantic Reading of *Don Quijote*," in *Critical Images: The Canonization of Don Quixote through Illustrated Editions of the Eighteenth Century* (Montreal: McGill-Queen's University Press, 1999); and Miguel de Unamuno, *Vida de Don Quijote y Sancho* (Madrid: Alianza Editorial, 1987).

7 | SHAKESPEARE'S QUIXOTE

Robin Chapman, *Shakespeare's Don Quixote* (London: Book Now, 2011); James Fitzmaurice-Kelly, *Cervantes and Shakespeare* (London: Oxford University Press, 1916); Javier Herrero, "Sierra Morena as Labyrinth: From Wilderness to Christian Knighthood," *Forum for Modern Language Studies*, 17 (1981): 55–67; Myriam Yvonne Jehenson, "The Dorotea-Fernando/Lucinda-Cardenio Episode in *Don Quijote*: A Postmodernist Play," *MLN*, 107 (1992): 205–9; Tomás Pabón, "Cardenio en Cervantes, Shakespeare y Fletcher," in *Actas del II Congreso Internacional de la Asociación de Cervantistas*, edited by Giuseppe Grilli (Naples, Italy: Instituto Universitario Orientale, 1995), pp. 371–78; and William Shakespeare and John Fletcher, *Cardenio, or*

SOURCES

The Second Maiden's Tragedy, edited by Charles Hamilton (Lakewood, Colorado: Glenbridge, 1994).

8 | THE EBULLIENT BUNCH

Mikhail Baryshnikov, *Baryshnikov: In Black and White* (New York: Bloomsbury, 2002); Walter Benjamin, "Franz Kafka: *Beim Bau der Chinesischen Mauer*," in *Selected Writings*, Vol. 2: *1927–1934*, translated by Rodney Livingstone et al., edited by Michael W. Jennings, Howard Eiland, and Gary Smith (Cambridge, Massachusetts: Harvard University Press, 1999), pp. 494–500; Jorge Luis Borges, "Parable of Cervantes and the *Quixote*," in *Labyrinths*, translated by James E. Irby (New York: New Directions, 1964); Lord Byron, *Don Juan*, edited by T. G. Steffan, E. Steffan, and W. W. Pratt, further readings by Susan J. Wolfson (New York: Penguin Classics, 1996); Anthony J. Cascardi, *The Bounds of Reason: Cervantes, Dostoevsky, Flaubert* (New York: Columbia University Press, 1986); Miguel de Cervantes, *Don Quijote de la Mancha*, ilustrated by Gustave Doré (Barcelona: Mundo Actual de Ediciones, 1981); Anthony J. Close, *The Romantic Approach to Don Quixote* (Cambridge: Cambridge University Press, 1978); Fyodor Dostoyevsky, *Complete Letters: 1878–1871*, edited by David A. Lowe (New York: Ardis, 1991); Dostoyevsky, *The Idiot*, translated by Richard Pevear and Larissa Volokhonsky (New York: Alfred A. Knopf, 2001); Dostoyevsky, *A Writer's Diary*, Vol. 2: *1877–1881*, translated and annotated by Kenneth Lantz (Evanston, Illinois: Northwestern University Press, 1994); Peter G. Earle, "In and Out of Time (Cervantes, Dostoevsky, Borges)," *Hispanic Review*, 71, no. 1 (2003): 1–13; Victor Espinós, *El "Quijote" en la música universal* (Barcelona: Instituto de Musicología, 1947); Bárbara Esquival-Heinemann, *Don Quijote's Sally into the World Opera: Libretti between 1680 and 1976* (New York: Land, 1993); Gustave Flaubert, *The Letters of Gustave Flaubert*, Vol. 1: *1830–1857*, and Vol. 2: *1857–1880*, selected, edited, and translated by Francis Steegmuller (Cambridge, Massachusetts: Harvard University Press, 1980); Flaubert, *Madame Bovary*, translated by Margaret Mauldon, introduction by Malcolm Bowie, notes by Mark Overstall (Oxford: Oxford University Press, 2004); Soledad Fox, *Flaubert and Don Quijote: The Influence of Cervantes on Madame Bovary* (Brighton,

England: Sussex Academic Press, 2008); Theodore Huebener, "Goethe and Cervantes," *Hispania*, 33, no. 2 (May 1950); Franz Kafka, "The Truth about Sancho Panza," in *The Collected Stories*, translated by Willa and Edwin Muir (New York: Schocken Books, 1971); Jules Massenet, *My Recollections* (New York: Greenwood, 1970); Rachel Schmidt, "The Romancing of *Don Quixote*: Spacial Innovation and Visual Interpretation in the Imaginiary of Johannot, Doré, and Daumier," *World and Image*, 14 (1998): 354–70; Arturo Serrano Plaja, *Realismo "mágico" en Cervantes: Don Quijote, visto desde Tom Sawyer y El Idiota* (Madrid: Gredos, 1967); David Thomson, *Rosebud: The Story of Orson Welles* (New York: Alfred A. Knopf, 1996); Alan Trueblood, "Dostoyevsky and Cervantes," *Inti*, 45 (1997): 85–94; and Rafael Utrera, "El Quijote en cine y televisión," *Ínsula* (1993): 558–59.

9 | AMERICA'S EXCEPTIONALISM

Hugh Henry Brackenridge, *Modern Chivalry*, Vol. 1: *Containing the Adventures of Captain John Farrago and Teague O'Regan, His servant*, edited by Claude M. Newin (Whitefish, Montana: Kessinger, 2007); Frank Brady, *Citizen Welles* (New York: Scribner, 1989); William Cullen Bryant, *The Poetical Works of William Cullen Bryant*, edited by Parke Godwin (2 vols.; New York: D. Appleton, 1883), vol. 2, p. 352; Simon Callow, *Orson Welles* (New York: Viking, 1996); Américo Castro, "Cervantes: The Orientation of Style," in *The Proper Study: Essays on Western Classics*, edited by Quentin Anderson and Joseph Anthony Mazzeo (New York: St. Martin's Press, 1962); John Dos Passos, *Travel Books and Other Writings: 1916–1941* (New York: Library of America, 2003); Manuel Durán, "El impacto de Cervantes en la obra de Twain," *Insula*, 661–62 (January–February 2002): 19–23; Joseph Ellis, *American Sphinx: The Character of Thomas Jefferson* (New York: Alfred A. Knopf, 1997); Ludwig Flato, editor, *Man of La Mancha: The Music Score* (New York: S. Fox, 1968); Montserrat Ginés, *The Southern Inheritors of Don Quixote* (Baton Rouge: Louisiana State University Press, 2000); Charles Haywood, "Musical Settings to Cervantes Texts," in *Cervantes across the Centuries: A Quadricentennial Volume*, edited by Angel Flores and M. J. Benardete (New York: Gordian Press, 1947), pp. 264–73; William Dean Howells, *My Literary Passions*, http://www.gutenberg

.org/cache/epub/3378/pg3378.html; Harry Levin, "*Don Quixote* and *Moby-Dick*," in *Cervantes across the Centuries: A Quadricentennial Volume*, edited by Angel Flores and M. J. Benardete (New York: Gordian Press, 1947), pp. 227–36; James Russell Lowell, *The Complete Writings of James Russell Lowell* (Boston: Houghton Mifflin, 1904); Herman Melville, *Moby-Dick: or, The Whale*, introduction by Andrew Delbanco, commentary by Tom Quirk (New York: Penguin Classics, 2002); Muppet Central, http://www.muppetcentral.com; George Santayana, "Tom Sawyer and Don Quixote," *Mark Twain Quarterly*, 9 (Winter 1952): 1–3; Freidhelm Schmidt-Welle and Ingrid Simson, editors, *El Quijote en América* (Amsterdam: Rodolphi, 2010); Susan Sontag, *Where the Stress Falls* (New York: Farrar, Straus & Giroux, 2001); Ilan Stavans and William P. Childers, "Tweeting at Windmills: *Don Quixote* in the Twenty-First Century," *Kenyon Review* Online, Winter 2015; John Steinbeck, *A Life in Letters*, edited by Elaine Steinbeck and Robert Wallsten (New York: Penguin Books, 1989); Mark Twain, *Adventures of Huckleberry Finn*, introduction by John Seelye, notes by Guy Cardwell (New York: Penguin Classics, 1985); Twain, *The Adventures of Tom Sawyer*, introduction by John Seelye, notes by Guy Cardwell (New York: Penguin Classics, 1986); Dale Wasserman, *The Impossible Musical: The "Man of la Mancha" Story* (New York: Applause, 2003); and Wasserman, with Joe Darion and Mitch Leigh, *Man of La Mancha: A Musical Play* (New York: Dell, 1969).

10 | FLEMISH TAPESTRIES·

J. A. G. Ardila, "Traducción y recepción del *Quijote* en Gran Bretaña (1612–1774)," *Anales Cervantinos*, 37 (2005): 253–65; Martin C. Battestin, "The Authorship of Smollett's *Don Quixote*," *Studies in Bibliography*, 50 (1997): 295–321; Julie Candler Hayes, "Tobias Smollett and the Translators of *Don Quijote*," *Huntington Library Quarterly*, 67, no. 4 (2004): 651–68; Miguel de Cervantes, *Don Quixote*, translated by J. M. Cohen (London: Penguin Classics, 1961); Cervantes, *Don Quixote*, translated by Edith Grossman, introduction by Harold Bloom (New York: Ecco, 2003); Cervantes, *Don Quixote*, translated by Charles Jarvis (New York: Washington Square Press, 1968); Cervantes, *Don Quixote*, edited by Tom Lathrop (New York: Signet, 2011);

Cervantes, *Don Quixote*, translated by James H. Montgomery (Cambridge, Massachusetts: Hackett, 2009); Cervantes, *Don Quixote*, translated by Peter Motteux, introduction by Stephen Boyd (London: Wordsworth Editions, 1992); Cervantes, *Histoire de l'admirable Don Quichotte de la Manche*, translated by François Filleau de Saint-Martin (1677); Cervantes, *The History and Adventures of the Renowned Don Quixote*, translated by Tobias Smollett, introduction by Carlos Fuentes (New York: Modern Library, 2001); Cervantes, *The History of Don Quixote of the Mancha*, translated by Thomas Shelton, introduction by James Fitzmaurice-Kelly (London: N. Nutt, 1896); Cervantes, *The Ingenious Hidalgo Don Quixote de la Mancha*, translated by Thomas Rutherford (London: Penguin, 2000); Robert Chambers, *Smollett: His Life and a Selection from His Writings* (London: W. & R. Chambers, 1867); Carmelo Cunchillos Jaime, "Traducciones inglesas del *Quijote*: la traducción de Motteux," *Cuadernos de investigación filológica*, 10, nos. 1–2 (1984): 111–28; Daniel Eisenberg, "The Text of *Don Quixote* as Seen by Its Modern English Translators," *Cervantes*, 26 (2006): 103–26; Lionel Kelly, editor, *Tobias Smollett: The Critical Heritage* (New York: Routledge, 1987); Edwin B. Knowles, "Thomas Shelton, Translator of *Don Quixote*," *Studies in the Renaissance*, 5 (1958): 160–75; Paula Luteran, *Six French and English Translations of Don Quixote Compared* (Lewiston, New York: Edwin Mellen Press, 2010); Michael J. McGrath, "Tilting at Windmills: *Don Quixote* in English," *Cervantes*, 26 (2006): 7–40; Lewis Melville, *The Life and Letters of Tobias Smollett (1721–1771)* (London: Faber & Gwyer, 1926); James H. Montgomery, "Was Thomas Shelton the Translator of the 'Second Part' (1620) of *Don Quixote*?," *Cervantes*, 26 (2006): 209–17; James Parr, "*Don Quixote*: Translation and Interpretation," *Philosophy and Literature*, 24, no. 2 (October 2000): 387–405; Ronald Paulson, *Don Quixote in England: The Aesthetics of Laughter* (Baltimore, Maryland: Johns Hopkins University Press, 1998); Anthony Pym, "The Translator as Author: Two Quixotes," *Translation and Literature*, 14 (2005): 71–81; Dale B. J. Randall and Jackson C. Boswell, *Cervantes in Seventeenth-Century England: The Tapestry Turned* (Oxford: Oxford University Press, 2009); Carmine Rocco Linsalata, *Smollett's Hoax: Don Quixote in English* (Stanford, California: Stanford University Press, 1956); G. S. Rousseau, *Tobias Smollett: Essays in Two Decades* (Edinburgh: T. & T. Clark, 1982);

Ilan Stavans, "*El 'Quijote'* en inglés," *El País Cultural* (Montevideo, Uruguay), no. 1121 (June 3, 2011): 6–7, translated into English in *A Critic's Journey* (Ann Arbor: University of Michigan Press, 2010), pp. 12–21; Stavans, "One Master, Many Cervantes," *Humanities*, 29, no. 5 (September–October 2008); Stavans, *Spanglish: The Making of a New American Language* (New York: HarperCollins, 2002); and Stavans, "The Translators of the *Quijote*," *Los Angeles Times* (December 14, 2003).

EPILOGUE

Donki, http://www.donki.com; Matthew Fraleigh, "El ingenioso samurai Don Kihote del Japón: Serizawa Keisuke's *A Don Quixote Picture Book*," *Review of Japanese Culture and Society* (December 2006): 87–120; and Ilan Stavans, *On Borrowed Words: A Memoir of Language* (New York: Viking, 2001).

INDEX

Note: *Italic* page numbers refer to illustrations.

250